A Theatre in the House

For my pupils,
the Friends of the Globe Theatre
and for my family

A THEATRE IN THE HOUSE

The Careys' Globe

ROSALIE CAREY

University of Otago Press

Published by the University of Otago Press
PO Box 56/56 Union Street, Dunedin, New Zealand
Fax: 64 3 479 8385
Email: university.press@stonebow.otago.ac.nz

List of Plays Performed at the Globe
© Katharina Ruckstuhl, 1999.
There may be small variations between this list
and the account given in the text.

Front cover photograph shows the post-performance party for
Romeo and Juliet, 1961. Left to right: Dallas Campbell, Patric Carey,
Rosalie Carey and Richard Butler. (Photograph courtesy de Clifford
James Photography.)
Back cover, top: Patric Carey, Betty Ussher, Paul Campbell,
Rosalie Carey and Aubrey Stephens take a break during the
Globe's construction.

Printed by GP Print Ltd, Wellington

Contents

?❧

Acknowledgements

ぁ

Having been at odds with arts councils almost all my professional life, it is really good to be able to express my sincere appreciation of the grant given me by the Queen Elizabeth II Arts Council Literature Committee, without which neither my physical nor my financial resources would have enabled me to write this book. Others have already written about Dunedin's Globe Theatre from an objective, academic point of view, but I write from the inside – my personal recollections and those of others closely connected with the Globe.

Writing the book has been both demanding and rewarding for me, but thanks to the grant I have been able to buy a computer and have sufficient tuition to use it – more or less. Reading through old programmes, newsletters and cuttings, to say nothing of talking to old friends, has reminded me of people and incidents long forgotten, and I marvel at the number of great roles many of our actors have played, and also the number of times others have appeared in tiny parts or worked backstage without recognition or obvious reward. Most of all I marvel at the achievement of Patric Carey, who built the greater part of the theatre himself; selected, directed and mounted an incredible list of plays; shared his pleasure in visual art, music and literature and somehow found time to decorate the house and tend the garden.

I would like to pay tribute to all those members, past and present, who have made the Globe what it is: a building that continues to change and improve, a place where plays and other artistic events happen regardless of box office returns. And I would like to thank the Hocken Library, Dunedin Public Library, the *Otago Daily Times*, and the various friends, with and without a capital F, particularly Marian Coxhead, Pamela Pow, John and Kathleen Dawson, Mickie Reid, and Prof. John Johnston, who have so generously given me their guidance and moral support. I am grateful to University of Otago Press and Marilyn Parker for their meticulous work on the text and their patience with my inefficiencies. I also thank Katharina Ruckstuhl for giving us the benefit of her research in the list of plays performed at the Globe and in checking personal names. Thanks, too, to Annette Facer, Polly Mason and Donald Reid for checking names. In a book of this nature, it is almost impossible to ensure every personal name or play title is rendered correctly. My apologies for any remaining inaccuracy.

The quotes I have chosen for *A Theatre in the House* include personal memories that friends who knew I was writing the book shared with me; many of the others, including those not otherwise described, are from *The Globe Theatre – a Celebration of 25 Years, 1961–1986*, a booklet edited by Marian Coxhead for the theatre's twenty-fifth birthday.

ROSALIE CAREY
Whangarei, May 1999

CHAPTER I

Small Frogs in a Big Puddle

Struggling in England

≈

The reconstruction of Shakespeare's Globe Theatre on the South Bank of the River Thames in London has been followed with interest by lovers of theatre and literature all over the world. But to many people in New Zealand, the Globe means a quaint little building at 104 London Street, in the Victorian city of Dunedin. It adjoins, and is partly incorporated into, what was a fine home built in 1864 by William Mason, the first mayor of Dunedin, and it was Niel Wales, a grandson of Mason's partner, who designed the original theatre almost a hundred years later.

The house is dominated by a huge magnolia tree. The perfume from its rich cream velvet blooms adds to the romance of approaching the theatre along a winding gravel path between flower-beds, overhanging trees, urns and statuary. Over the years the roots of this tree have done untold damage to the once-elegant house. I say 'once-elegant' for it is now in a sorry state of repair and its future is uncertain.

Following the Masons, the Begg family of music-store fame occupied the house until the fifties, when it was rented out and ultimately became sufficiently run-down to be purchased by an impecunious theatrical couple – my ex-husband, Patric Carey, and myself.

The theatre's exterior does little to excite the eye, its special feature being the domed neo-octagonal roof devised to give maximum height without the use of pillars. The interior, on the other hand, was such that when it opened in 1961, the theatre was as like an Elizabethan playhouse as possible, given the current research, the restrictions of by-laws, the shape of the section, and cost. The structural features and the fact that it was created by people who would work in it, made the name 'Globe' the obvious choice.

The building has undergone many changes since its inception. Indeed, much had to happen in our lives before it could even be contemplated, for we knew no wealthy patrons and had no money of our own. Our only assets were a will to work, and valuable experience both in small underfunded professional theatres in England and New Zealand, and in teaching theatre-related skills. Perhaps, even more importantly, we shared a belief in plays of merit rather than box office successes.

It would be false to suggest that we had always dreamed of having a building to work in that actually belonged to us. It was more the result of circumstance than planning, but it had far-reaching effects, as David Carnegie, an outside observer of the Globe and later Head of Drama Studies at Victoria University, recognised in 1984:

> Patric and Rosalie Carey and the Globe Theatre have had an influence on Dunedin Theatre out of all proportion to the small numbers of people who went to see the plays. Scorned and ignored by the establishment and idolized by much of the artistic and intellectual community, the Careys confronted the city with a philosophy of theatre that placed the imaginative creation of the playwright above all else.

> Box-office returns, production standards, even the audience took second place to the idea of the play and the actor's encounter with it. The Globe always felt itself a beleaguered bastion of creativity in a land of Philistines, and it inevitably made bitter enemies as well as loyal friends. But when Patric Carey retired in 1973 after fifteen idiosyncratic years of almost single-handed theatre, he had proved to Dunedin that theatre could be more than entertainment.

For us that 'second place' also included our own well-being and that of our children. For the Globe was not only unplanned, it was born prematurely as well.

So, how did it come about? And why did it happen in Dunedin? Before leaving England in 1953 we had been warned that if we wanted to start anything in New Zealand it must not be in Dunedin, which Dame Sybil Thorndyke had labelled 'the graveyard of theatre'. Here then, are some of the circumstances that eventually led us to have a 'Theatre in the House'.

When I was growing up in the country near Lumsden in the far South, and then in Hamilton in the North Island, there was virtually no outlet for artistic expression of any kind other than what we created ourselves. I was almost unique in having lessons in 'elocution', music, and dancing and frequently entertained at clubs and concerts. In my teens a school friend and I took part in one-act play festivals and also attended readings of full-length plays with the WEA (Workers' Education Association), where we learnt to appreciate quality drama.

Shortly after leaving school I dramatised two novels which, with the help of my family and friends, were produced on a grand scale with Hamilton's best actors, music specially composed for a locally assembled orchestra, and costumes hired from Wellington. It caused quite a stir in a town that normally accepted nothing but West End comedies. Then, after setting up as a teacher of speech and drama, followed by three-and-a-half years in the Air Force, I was offered my fare to England by a maiden aunt – a professional watercolour artist who liked (at least in the holidays) to have her nieces share her tiny cottage in St Ives in Cornwall. My aunt was a member of the St Ives artist's colony and through her I met Ben Nicholson, Harry Rowntree, Misomé Pelle and Daphne du Maurier. She also took her nieces with her when she went abroad, at enormous financial sacrifice to herself.

Throughout World War II, I had dreamed of training in London, and so with my aunt's help I enrolled at the Guildhall School of Music and Drama, starting in February 1946. There I added a licentiate diploma to my fellowship with the Trinity College of London. By a miracle, just as funds ran out I was engaged to understudy the leading lady and play 'as cast' with the Adelphi Guild Theatre, an excellent Arts Council-backed company whose work I had admired.

For the next few years I worked in a variety of companies, including weekly repertory as leading lady, and a tiny fringe theatre in London. I was second-lead in a touring musical, and did a summer season on the Isles of Scilly, where seven of us acted, directed, made costumes, built sets, did the publicity, and even made our own spotlights. All this we did for eleven weeks for the princely sum of £4/5/- a week – a little less than the Equity minimum.

As well as acting and working behind the scenes I found theatrical 'digs' on touring dates an education in themselves. Some were positively luxurious but others simply had a hip-bath with water heated once a week in the wash-house copper. One row of houses we stayed in had no toilets – just chamber pots under the beds and communal loos at the end of the block. In one billet, the toilet stood unashamedly right beside the gas stove.

In contrast with my sheltered life in New Zealand, the stress of working in the theatre – and more particularly not working – took its toll, and by the end of one long engagement I was ordered three months' rest.

When I began the job search again only about one actor in ten was working, but towards the end of 1949 I was engaged by the English

Ring Actors based in Penzance, who brought really well-presented plays to a circuit of West-Cornish towns including St Ives. I was to double as a maid, and the sexy young wife of an elderly roué, played by the company's designer. Because he was also busy creating the sets for the Christmas pantomime and I was commuting from St Ives, we did not meet until the dress rehearsal. All I knew of him was the stage manager's complaints about 'Paddy and his ruddy great sets'!

I had seen this mysterious gentleman in his black overcoat and beret, paint bespattered shoes, longish hair, and goatee beard, in the street and at the theatre. He always carried an interesting cane and was invariably on his own. When we did meet I found him very shy but charming, and was impressed with his pleasing voice, gentle wit and lively blue eyes. It was only in that company that he was called 'Paddy'. His real name was Patric Carey.

We found we had a good deal in common and spent as much time as possible together. He told me that although he enjoyed designing and building sets, his real vocation was as a director – not of box office rubbish, but plays by great dramatists: plays that had something to say about, and to, society. His eyes lit up when I told him I was planning to return to New Zealand, as soon as finances allowed, to establish a studio where I could train actors with a view to establishing a professional theatre company. I dreamt of a centre where performing and visual artists and musicians could study, without the trauma I had experienced of travelling to the other side of the world.

At the end of the season with the English Ring Actors Patric asked me to marry him – conditional, of course, upon his finding another job. A proposal of marriage was hardly what I had expected from this man, and he was not exactly what I had expected in a husband; but I so enjoyed his company and his original ideas and talents, I did not wish to lose sight of him. Besides, I claimed I was tired of being chaste!

I had been pursued by other men. In fact, when the chance to work in Penzance came up it was doubly acceptable as it enabled me to escape not only a dreary job (dictaphone typist for Kodak Ltd) but also from the attentions of an amorous Pole who, much to the envy of the five other eligible females, had frequently joined me while on tour.

Much earlier in New Zealand, soon after I had left school, I met and fell in love with an interesting man many years my senior who was visiting Hamilton. We carried on a lively correspondence for several years, but when we met again I was so shy I could barely utter a word;

and when his hand went up my skirt I fled. Inevitably he turned his attentions elsewhere, and I was devastated.

Then, among others, there was the tall, dark and handsome Englishman serving with the New Zealand Air Force who proposed unsuccessfully before he went overseas with the Air Force. After I had been in England about six months, one dozen red roses arrived from Harrods every Monday for six weeks. I knew they were not from the nice young man I was going out with at the time and so was extremely puzzled until 'tall, dark and handsome' arrived on my doorstep from New Zealand. We went abroad and to the Lake District, closely chaperoned by my aunt. He subsequently bought me a beautiful diamond ring and we announced our engagement in *The Times*.

At the time I left New Zealand waiting lists were so long that anyone wanting a permit to travel was obliged to sign a document saying they would not ask to return to New Zealand for two years. However, my friend managed to work his passage home. After a while we both realised and agreed by letter that we were not really suited. We remained good friends even after both of us were married.

Although Patric and I spent twenty-five years together I still know little about his past, other than that his family came from the West of Ireland. His father was killed when he and his only sister were very young, resulting in extreme financial hardship. Patric, however, received a sound education from Jesuit priests, but to his constant regret had to leave school at an early age to earn a living.

He spent all his spare time reading and, having a photographic memory, acquired a phenomenally wide knowledge on a variety of subjects, particularly those related to the arts. The turning point in his youthful career was seeing Micheál MacLiammóir in Oscar Wilde's *The Importance of Being Earnest*. He decided to become an actor. At seventeen he joined Lord Longford's touring company, and later went to England to play in small troupes doing weekly, sometimes twice-nightly repertory, or touring one-night stands.

Throughout the six years of World War II he served with the RAF first as a glider pilot and then with a radar unit that took him to Burma for three-and-a-half years, much of which time was spent behind the lines, living in the jungle or sheltering in foxholes with bombs dropping all around.

Fortunately he was with a remarkable little group of men, all but one of whom were university graduates and all of whom had an interest in the arts. After the war, they pooled their resources and formed a theatre company on the Isle of Wight. They were based in Ventnor and toured to other centres. Patric was the only one with any true theatrical experience but he had a gift for nurturing natural talent. The company was successful until the British Arts Council elected to set up a resident company in Shanklin, their most profitable touring date, an action that no doubt coloured Patric's attitude towards arts councils in general.

After that he worked with a variety of companies as director, designer or both. One engagement, at Basingstoke, proved a disaster. The management absconded leaving Patric to pay off the debts. He returned to London with enough money for a loaf of bread and a packet of cigarettes that had to last him a week. Little wonder that at the end of 1949, much as he hated watching others direct, he was grateful for an engagement as designer with the English Ring Actors in Penzance.

When the season ended we made the usual pilgrimage back to London. After weeks of subsistence living, Patric met a friend who told him that a new company was to spend the summer at the Pavilion Theatre in Penzance, and the manager wanted the designer who had worked there with the English Ring Actors. It was not directing as Patric had hoped but he was guaranteed a couple of productions, and in the theatre even the top echelon cannot always be choosers.

Our marriage took place on Midsummer Day 1951 in the beautiful little church, with roses round the door, at Gulval, midway between Penzance and St Ives. With us were Aunt Helen, two friends of hers who actually had a car, and the stage manager, who drove Patric to the ceremony in the company truck. Our three-day honeymoon was on the Isles of Scilly where we stayed in the romantic-looking Star Castle Hotel, built by Napoleon in the shape of a star. The proprietress gave us special rates in recognition of 'the pleasure she had had from the repertory season on the island'.

My most poignant recollection of the honeymoon was sitting on a huge rock in the sun while Patric recited the first two acts of *Hamlet*, which he regarded as the greatest murder story in the English language. He had directed a shortened version for the university in Rangoon, but longed to present it in its entirety. But there seemed little chance of this, especially if we remained in England.

We dreamed of being able to work together. To this end Patric applied for – but did not get – the directorship of a tiny company in

Truro in Cornwall. The interview was on a wet and windy day. The only memorable feature of the expedition was a gust of wind ripping Patric's ageing raincoat from hem to collar, and a second gust throwing it over the side of a bridge into the river below. Its replacement was one I bought from another actress whose brother had died of starvation following the collapse of a tour in Canada.

I accompanied Patric to Cromer for his next engagement but he remained in London while I went to Grantham as leading lady for a limited season. In a moment of extreme optimism – or perhaps desperation – we put our names down for passages to New Zealand. Then, as winter approached and we were at our lowest ebb, my dear Aunt Helen offered to lend us the money for the fares.

I made a last-ditch round of agents, a depressing business as most of them were in dreary little offices up three or four flights of stairs. At the door of one of these dens two young people were leaving.

'Back to the pease pudding,' I heard one of them say. 'We eat on alternate days. On the other, we stay in bed!'

I wondered if this was to be my fate as well; but the agent said, 'Come in, Miss Seddon.' (I still used my maiden name professionally.) 'You've been with the Adelphi Guild Theatre. You could be just the person I'm looking for.'

The engagement was with the much-respected Caryl Jenner Company. As well as a programme for schools, they were touring *The Holly and the Ivy* by John Wynyard and I was to play one of the Aunts. I had four days to learn the part, but the miraculous thing was that the tour took us to Cornwall. By travelling in the back of the van with the properties, with no light and little air Patric was able to come with us, and we had Christmas together in St Ives with my aunt.

We said goodbye to England on a cold foggy day in 1953 not unlike the one when I arrived just over seven years before. We enjoyed the sea voyage immensely, even though we had only £30 spending money to last the two of us five weeks. Fortunately most of the bright young people who became our friends on board were similarly placed. One young man, who was taking up a junior lectureship in classics, reached this country with threepence in his pocket.

We had resolved to make the trip a reading and resting time, but were cajoled into taking part in the deck games at which we failed spectacularly. Then we were asked to arrange the ship's concert. Rather than the usual dreary string of items, we devised a revue, largely with original material, that proved a great success.

I did not want the voyage to end but it was exciting to be coming home at last. We had no idea what the future might have in store for us, but I felt that, whatever else, I was a competent actress and would be an enthusiastic teacher of speech and drama. I also hoped the difficult years in England had equipped me with something to bring back for New Zealand theatre. But regardless of what I could offer myself, I was bringing Patric Carey.

Above: Rosalie Carey, London 1947.
Below: Rosalie as Marini in Lilac
Time, *touring production, England,*
September 1949.
Left: Patric Carey when first in
Dunedin.

Production of Women of Troy, *by Euripides. Performed in garden of Ashburn Hall, 1959.*

CHAPTER II

Big Frogs in a Small Puddle

A new start in New Zealand

જ

During the voyage out a fellow traveller, Dr John Pocock, had told us that his friends Richard and Edith Campion were planning to start a theatre company. We paid little attention at the time, but on our arrival in New Zealand in early February 1953, splashed across the *New Zealand Herald* was the news that the Campions were that very day launching a professional theatre company generously funded by the Hannah Trust (Edith is a member of the Hannah family). This was the tremendously exciting but short-lived New Zealand Players.

Their first production was fully cast, but our friends had already made arrangements for us to meet with the Director of CAS (Community Arts Service) which operated under the auspices of the Adult Education Branch of Auckland University, taking plays, opera, ballet and music to small as well as larger venues throughout the North Island.

The next production, Somerset Maugham's *The Circle,* was almost cast, but they had kept a small part for me, while Patric was to be stage director in charge of the tour. The founder-director, Harold Baigent, was going overseas. Patric would 'learn the ropes' and take over the next production. What could be better? Two salaries, however small, and an opportunity to see the whole of the North Island, were not to be sneezed at.

By the end of two tours we had engagements lined up in Hamilton and Wellington. The Wellington Repertory production was an excellent play, *The River Line* by Charles Morgan. Apart from the leading man being too drunk to perform on the second night, leaving Patric to take his place with the book in his hand, it was an unquestioned success.

Living in Wellington was horribly expensive. The minimum wage was eleven pounds a week and we were paying fourteen each for bed and breakfast. On the Monday morning after *The River Line* production, two envelopes were pushed under the door. They were our bank statements. Both accounts were in the red. There was no definite work in sight for either of us and I was pregnant. Nevertheless, we decided to live in the capital.

Eventually we were lucky enough to find a charming flat near the city centre at a remarkably good rate. It belonged to Dr Cyril and Irene Adcock who were to spend a year in England. They left their nineteen-year-old daughter (later to become the successful novelist Marilyn Duckworth) with a girlfriend in the flatlet above. We established an immediate rapport with the Adcocks, and Irene became a very special friend to me, and later to the Globe Theatre.

Once settled we put out an impressive brochure announcing ourselves as the New Zealand Academy of Theatre Arts and soon had a good number of pupils. I was invited to teach speech one day a week at Marsden College. There was work with radio drama from time to time, as well as adjudications and productions through the Theatre Federation and the British Drama League. Our future seemed assured.

Before leaving England Patric had qualified as a member of the Guild of Drama Adjudicators and shortly after our arrival was asked to officiate in Hamilton, where I was still remembered. From then on he was much in demand, and festivals often led to engagements up and down the country. At home we enjoyed a round of parties, mayoral receptions, and after-show gatherings for visiting artists. Patric was a great success artistically and socially.

Mid-year I was invited to direct a play for the British Drama League Festival with a group of five women. We became good friends and they asked if, after my baby was born, they could come to our flat on Thursday evenings for tuition in drama. This class became very important to me, as I was lonely with Patric away so much. He was billeted in fine homes, and wined and dined wherever he went. In Gore, where there was plenty of money but little entertainment, life was particularly good. When he came home he was starry eyed. His first words were 'Too many parties'.

Our son Christopher was born in October 1954. By a stroke of good fortune, Patric was in Wellington directing *Alice in Wonderland* for the Repertory Society, with Molly Cook's fabulous costumes and a brilliant cast – Selwyn Toogood and his brother Neville playing Tweedle-dum and Tweedle-dee, with Neville's wife Dorothy as Alice. As well we had Marie Jones (who later played a prominent role in *Flying Doctors* in Australia), Barbara Basham (Aunt Daisy's daughter),

Eileen Teward, Kevin Woodall, Kenneth Adams, and David Tinkham. Leigh Brewer was the choreographer and John Ritchie of Christchurch composed the music which was played by an ensemble headed by Alex Lindsay. Desmond Digby did one superb set; Patric did the others. It was a truly magnificent production. Wellington was bristling with talent and there were audiences and money to support it. How much easier it would have been for us if we had continued working there!

When the time came to leave the Adcocks', John Gordon of broadcasting fame lent us his flat for the six weeks he was on tour with the New Zealand Players. Then we found a big upstairs apartment, right in the city on the corner of Willis and Vivian Streets. Here the studio and 'The Thursdays' as we now called my drama group, flourished. Husbands, sons, and boyfriends joined our classes, and took part in poetry readings and plays.

We were in the planning stages of 'The Thursdays' first three-act play (Noel Coward's *Quiet Weekend)* for which we had booked the Concert Chamber, when we were visited by the president of the Dunedin Repertory Society. Patric had been a great success adjudicating in the city, and had obviously impressed Cecile Trevor, a driving force in the theatre, and it was Cecile's idea that the society, which had fallen on hard times, could be saved if they engaged a professional producer.

The president offered Patric a year's contract, with autonomy in the choice of play and all possible assistance. Membership was dropping daily, there were only four men on the books, they were four hundred pounds in debt, and at the annual general meeting had failed to get a quorum. However, a private sponsor had come up with enough money for a basic salary, which could be augmented with freelance work. I had everything going for me in Wellington and was reluctant to leave, but it meant so much for Patric to have a steady income, however small, that of course we accepted.

Dunedin had the red carpet down for us – huge splashes in the newspapers, parties in the newly decorated Repertory rooms, and a succession of teas with elderly ladies at the women's club. Everything was fine as long as the current committee stayed in office.

We stayed with Cecile and John Trevor while we looked for a place of our own. We had nearly settled for a most unsuitable flat when we were offered the former home of the late Willi Fels – New Zealand's first German Consul – a man of great wealth and culture who had contributed largely to the Otago Museum. The new owner of 84 London Street had furnished it with rich carpets and antique furniture, and offered it to us at a remarkably reasonable rent complete with gardener.

The grounds had been extensive with native bush, lawns and statuary. One piece – presumably Clio, goddess of history, for she was reading (anachronistically) a bound book – was still in our part of the garden, which had long ago been subdivided. Originally there had been all nine muses as well as a handsome pergola supported by classic columns. Later, I was able to purchase Clio for a ridiculously small sum as a birthday present for Patric, and when the Globe was built she was housed in the foyer.

When possible Patric went away directing or adjudicating. I took a few pupils, the first being Gabrielle Johnston, aged ten. She had private or group lessons once a week and later came regularly to classes as well as taking part in plays, till she went overseas ten years later.

One member of the staff at St Hilda's Collegiate School, who had taught me English and French at the Hamilton High School, remembered my work as an actress and teacher. On her recommendation I was invited to teach speech on an extra-curricular basis three days a week in the senior school. I found it very tiring and often had problems arranging care for Christopher, but it was also very rewarding, particularly working with the young girls from the country, and it gave us a small but secure income for the next nine years. Later I took whole classes, and the results endorsed my belief that every child should be given the opportunity of having basic speech training if the effective use of the English language is to be maintained.

Rilla Stephens, a lovely actress who had recently returned to Dunedin after studying at the Old Vic School in London, was eager to use her vast knowledge and skills working alongside people who had our kind of practical experience. We were delighted. The three of us conducted tremendously popular drama classes on Saturday mornings, working on movement and style for period plays, voice production, characterisation, and literature; and we experimented with creative drama – a relatively new concept. The classes brought in very little money because our private pupils and Repertory Society members came free. But we three tutors all learnt from each other and felt we had plenty to offer our students. Among other things Rilla did a stylish production of *Gamma Gurton's Needle,* first in the wonderful reception rooms at 84 London Street, and then for the Drama League festival.

Imagine our chagrin when, at about twelve o'clock one night while Patric was working alone on a set, the new president of the Repertory Society dropped in after a committee meeting to complain that our drama classes were not what they should be. Young people, according to him, should be sitting around reading plays.

Inspired by a flat lawn at the bottom of our garden with terraces and steps leading down to it, we decided we must do a Greek play. Our idea was to do it under the aegis of the Repertory Society, but they would have none of it, even though it would not interfere in any way with their regular programme.

Their conservatism was getting Patric down. So we went ahead on our own with Euripides' *Medea* with Bertha Rawlinson and Lindsay Campbell in the leads. The New Zealand Players were in Dunedin at the time and several of them came to see the production on a particularly beautiful Sunday afternoon. They were ecstatic about it. Richard Campion admitted to having been reduced to tears.

We were invited to take *Medea* to Invercargill where an over-zealous promoter billed it as 'the greatest love story ever told', and was disgusted that I, who had taken over the part of the Nurse at the last minute, wore flat shoes and a totally unflattering costume whereas he had expected me to provide a bit of glamour.

We also played to a full house in the new community hall in Alexandra. Carried away by our success we became more venturesome and decided to bring the show to the general public in Dunedin. We had planned to use the Concert Chamber, but it was undergoing renovations and the only available venue was His Majesty's Theatre. This involved enormous expense. Bertha's husband, Stuart Falconer, offered to put up £500 and we blithely went ahead; but alas, we were left with a £300 debt, a burden from which we never really recovered.

Throughout the year the Repertory Society went from strength to strength. By Christmas membership was approaching five hundred with a healthy proportion of males, their £400 debt was now a credit of equal size, and Patric's engagement was extended for a further three months.

Unfortunately, the new committee was more commercially minded, and Patric's autonomy in choice of play was steadily eroded. At this late stage he was asked to sign a contract. He pointed out to the president, who happened to be a lawyer and chairman of twenty-nine committees, that two of the clauses contradicted each other. The said gentleman was furious. The main problem, however, was the restriction on Patric undertaking other engagements in the area, and the salary was ridiculously small.

At the annual general meeting Patric told the members that if he was expected to direct the plays, build and paint the sets, collect and return properties, do the publicity, and arrange social evenings – quite apart from the weekly drama classes – he might have to resign.

The president, who was brilliant at pushing through an agenda said, 'Resignation accepted,' and declared the meeting closed. It transpired that, presumably over drinks, he had offered the position to Graeme Clifford, a visiting opera singer, who had little or no experience of producing straight plays.

Graeme had had an introduction to us during his tour with Gilbert and Sullivan operas. We had enjoyed his company enormously. Imagine his embarrassment when he visited us later, and found he had unwittingly accepted Patric's job.

For three years we scraped a living teaching, adjudicating, conducting seminars, and producing plays in and around Dunedin on a freelance basis – in halls, churches, gardens, the university quadrangle, among the rocks at Alexandra, and in the Cine Club Theaterette – keeping just one jump ahead of the creditors.

One of Patric's early engagements in Gore had been to rescue a production of an enthusiastic, talented but relatively inexperienced director – a lawyer by the name of Bernard Esquilant. He and William (Bill) Menlove, a young farmer from Lumsden with some financial resources and a keen interest in amateur theatre, won a Drama League Competition and were so excited by this that they decided to turn professional. They worked out a sound plan to tour box office comedies to the little places in the South Island that would never see the New Zealand Players, and invited Patric to direct for them – at 'mates' rates' of course.

We were most sympathetic and spent hours, if not days, answering questions and making suggestions. They had not, for instance, thought of playing for schools. They needed a cast and there were very few people in 1957 prepared to give up a steady job in order to go 'on the road', especially with an untried group.

However, between our friends in Dunedin and others from Wellington we assembled an excellent company – the Southern Comedy Players – for whose first production Patric chose Brandon Thomas's evergreen *Charley's Aunt*. To save money, Patric designed and built most of the set himself. It was a polished production but touring is not easy, especially if most of the company are more experienced than the management. We met up with them in Invercargill, where it transpired that the company was on the point of collapse. Patric cajoled and placated the cast and the tour continued, but the dissension in the company had already done it great disservice.

Rilla Stephens had meanwhile joined the New Zealand Players for a tour of *A Midsummer Night's Dream*, as Titania. Finding herself out of work at the end of the season she and John Hunter, who had played Puck, conceived the idea of taking out a tour of Noel Coward's *Private Lives* with Patric as their director. Rather than start a new company, Patric came up with a strategy that proved highly successful.

Bernard and Bill were on tour but we eventually tracked them down, and phoned them. They had no definite plans for the future, so with Rilla, John, and me giggling in the background Patric told them he had a proposition. Why not do *Private Lives* with Rilla Stephens and Johnny Hunter in the leads? They would be an undoubted box office draw, and he believed that if he played his cards right, etc etc.

The ruse worked and it was an excellent production, with a stylish set designed and largely executed by Patric, though owing to friction between him and Bernard he was given no credit for it on the programme.

We were thinking about the third production when Patric met Bernard in the street and learnt that it was to be Douglas Home's *Sailor Beware*. Patric asked who would play the Peggy Mount part, which required a mature comedy actress. Bernard apparently had someone in mind, and little more was said. Shortly afterwards it was announced that Graeme Clifford would direct the play.

It was a matter of considerable pride to us that we had made possible the first indigenous professional company in the South Island, and we had had great hopes of co-operation with Bernard and Bill in terms of interchange of expertise and casts, while we worked in the city and they continued to tour. What would be our future now? There was no hope of work with the Repertory Society, and little chance of professional engagements elsewhere.

Just before the August school holidays we learned that 84 London Street was on the market, and I found myself pregnant again. Little wonder that rumours went round that the Careys were leaving Dunedin, to say nothing of the surprise expressed when, thanks to help from my family and a favourable loan from the Otago Savings Bank, we bought our own home one block further up the hill.

No. 104 London Street was a property we felt had real potential. The downstairs rooms were full of junk, but one was a good size for a studio. We kept the charming tenants who had been in the upstairs flat for years and who enjoyed looking after the garden. By making a bedsitting room for ourselves and putting Christopher in what had been the pantry, we could manage. Leaving the city would have been admitting defeat, and in any case we had no money to start elsewhere. If nothing else, I had a steady job at St Hilda's College, we had a good following among the young people, and we had each other.

While we were still falling over a circular saw in the breakfast room, we were invited to a post-tour party with the Southern Comedy Players. Bernard and Bill had also acquired an old home, but theirs had been beautifully refurbished to their excellent taste, by professional labour.

One day towards the end of 1957, while I was at school, a call came for me at morning break. A voice said, 'This is the casting committee of Rosalie and Patric Carey Productions. You are required to play Clytaemnestra in the *Trilogy of the Oresteia* of Aeschylus for Festival Week at the end of January.'

This was typical of Patric's way of working. He had been having coffee with our good friend Betty Dodds when he learned that Bertha Rawlinson, who was to have been a major drawcard as the lead, was no longer available because of a commitment to the Repertory Society. Patric and Betty decided I should play this extremely demanding role. His reason for such an ambitious choice as the *Oresteia* was that since New Zealand had no tradition in theatre he must give it one: he would present every possible great play interspersed with exciting new ones. (Maori culture was still being ignored, especially in the South Island.)

For the *Oresteia* he enlisted the co-operation of the classics and music departments of the university, and on Dr Guy Manton's suggestion we used a translation by Sir John Shephard who had been Guy's tutor at Cambridge University. This version had not been performed in public before and the old man was so delighted that he put himself on a ship and came all the way from England to see it.

Finding twelve men for the chorus of elders was quite an exercise. I spent hours on the telephone and in the process discovered some significant talent, not the least of which was nineteen-year-old Ian Ralston who, one year later, gave a remarkable performance in the title role of Sophocles' *Oedipus Rex*. Alternating daily with *Antigone* in the Cine Club at 5.30 p.m. these two plays unexpectedly drew our best audiences to date.

Being in the chorus of a Greek play was a splendid initiation for new actors. They learnt how to move freely and how to stand still, to say nothing of how to project their voices, since most of these productions were performed in the open air.

All through rehearsals of the *Oresteia* I had extreme difficulty in concentrating. There were so many other demands on my time – preparing my work for the college and the studio, making curtains and covering furniture for our home, helping with costumes, collecting advertisements for the programme, and generally acting as production secretary. It was a while since I had learnt a long part, and pregnancy didn't help. The first performance was to have been in the Medlicotts' beautiful garden, but heavy rain forced us to move into Allen Hall at the university.

When the moment came for my first entrance I was so unbelievably nervous I had to be pushed onto the stage. Sir John's words floated away from me like Agamemnon's fleet. When I apologised to the old gentleman for rewriting his text he graciously said it was so long since he wrote it that he hadn't really noticed. His only criticism was that perhaps I didn't bring out the *maternal* side of Clytaemnestra's character!

Medea and *Oresteia* were only the beginning. All in all Patric produced nineteen Greek plays himself, I produced three and Ian Ralston one. Although Patric did considerable research as to the modus operandi of the ancient Greeks, we made no attempt to emulate them exactly but developed a style of our own. Our favourite translators were Fitts and Fitzgerald who proved how modern, daring and, in the case of the comedies, how hilariously funny the Greeks could be.

My generation was introduced to the Greeks via Granville Barker but when, much later in 1971, I asked my adult students to read his translation of *Hippolytus* (along with others for comparison) they found Barker's style so quaint that I produced it with them as a 'send up'. We had a particularly tall Theseus and a very small Hippolytus, a contrast we highlighted with the use of a rostrum. Pillars fell down at crucial moments and when a 'tablet' was mentioned we produced the Catholic newspaper of that name.

For *Electra* (the second play of the *Trilogy of the Oresteia*) and Aristophanes' *The Birds*, Anne de Roo, who had already proved herself a competent dramatist with a one-act play in the genre of the Theatre of the Absurd, and a verse drama commissioned for CORSO, provided us with clever translations. Like its progenitor, Anne's version of *The*

Birds satirised well-known contemporary personalities quite unashamedly.

Not long before, Bruce Mason had brought his first solo show to Dunedin. One of the best audience responses to our production of *The Birds* came on the lines 'It's clouding over', to which the reply from John Fairmaid as Bruce Mason was, 'Yes it does look like the end of the golden weather.' At that moment the sun went behind a cloud.

Sometimes we experimented with masks, in particular for the Furies in *The Eumenidies* (part three of *Oresteia)* and larger than life papier-mâché ones for the gods in *Alcestis*. It was exciting to discover how much these masks enhanced the resonance of voices, especially when we played in a field in Alexandra with the gods high up on enormous rocks.

Dunedin's Festival Week was instituted to attract people back to the city at the end of January when most of them had fled the unsatisfactory summer weather. Other than one concert by the National Orchestra (as the New Zealand Symphony Orchestra was called then) there was no live entertainment. Rehearsals could be difficult with so many people out of town, but on the plus side we had free advertising in brochures and newspapers along with other festival events and could hope for a little financial return after the long Christmas holidays when there was no other income.

My baby was born on 5 July 1958. At the time I was not only carrying on with my normal teaching at home and at St Hilda's but I was also in the midst of a school production of Shakespeare's *Much Ado About Nothing*. Patric agreed to take over the pupils and the play for the last few weeks, but as it happened he had an engagement to direct a musical comedy in Invercargill and so was away much of the time. I had no choice but to keep on working till the very last minute. By chance Patric came home for a weekend one week ahead of schedule and Belinda conveniently chose to arrive prematurely at the same time.

I had had a comfortable pregnancy and the birth was a little easier than the first one. Even so I was thoroughly sedated and regretted that, once again, I had failed to have a natural birth and this time could not breast feed. Fortunately Belinda was a healthy, contented baby. On the days I was in the classroom, dear Betty Dodds acted as nurse-girl, at first at our place and after a few weeks at her own. A taxi driver would take the baby in the carry-cot with the money for the fare and her bottles tucked in the blankets. Other days Belinda would come with me to the school and remain in the pram in the studio or be trusted to the kitchen staff who loved to play Nanny to her. When I was teaching at home she would be parked discreetly behind the desk.

Once when a bunch of us were making costumes in our breakfast room, someone asked if they could see the baby. Belinda had disappeared. She was finally found in her bassinet with her head pushed under the table and a pile of period costumes dumped on her feet!

Both children came with us to Burns Hall when we had productions there. For Shakespeare's *The Taming of the Shrew* and for *Hamlet* (which we did in its entirety) Patric built Jacobean-type stages with balconies, staircases and thrust stages beyond the existing proscenium arch. He had no workshop and these edifices were constructed on the far-from-flat area at the side of the house (or in our sitting room), and taken to the hall in pieces.

When we did John Webster's *The Duchess of Malfi*, the weather was bad so the building took place in the big studio – our drawing room. Pat Harrison and Raewyn Lamb alternated playing the Duchess and it was at a rehearsal, in that confined space, that Pat gave a magical performance that resulted in a stunned silence, followed by spontaneous clapping.

In *Hamlet* Reg Graham was an impressive Prince of Denmark, Ophelia was played on alternate nights by Jenepher Harty and Rozena Hallam (one of my first pupils and now a successful teacher, director, and professional actor in Christchurch). The small part of Osric was brought to life by a talented young student, Grant Tilly, who has since become a household name in Wellington theatre.

Both the *Otago Daily Times* and the *Evening Star* were loud in their praise of the acting, the direction, the costumes and music and 'the amazing effect of seeing a Shakespeare play for the first time on a two-tiered stage ...'

But at that time Dunedin was indifferent. Even the schools did not consider a live production of *Hamlet* worthy of their attention.

Having discovered the advantages of presenting Shakespeare on a two-tiered stage, I decided I must have one for *Much Ado About Nothing* and Patric obliged. But when he came to erect it, it was half-an-inch too tall. We were devastated. Unperturbed, the headmistress contacted a member of the board who was in the furniture trade and in no time professional carpenters had everything under control. I could not help wondering why Patric had expended all that precious effort in the first place. Like so many young mothers I felt perpetually tired and overworked but having already suffered from burn-out I tried to pace myself. Patric, however, had yet to learn that human energy is not an unlimited resource.

Post-war England was understandably conventional as the population searched for normality. Most London theatres continued to present box office thrillers and light comedies, relying for their appeal on star performances. Fortunately for the serious theatregoer, there was the Old Vic Company's brilliant season of Shakespeare and other classics. It was not surprising that the most exciting new voice on the London scene was Christopher Fry, a prolific, imaginative wordmonger. *The Lady's Not for Burning* hit the West End like daffodils in spring.

Post-war French theatre was directed at the bourgeoisie – even though, back in 1896, Jouvet had written that he saw life as being totally illogical and language inadequate for communication. The saviour for mankind, he maintained, was laughter. To prove his point he produced off-beat plays in his own private theatre. Then in 1953 Paris saw the first production of *Waiting for Godot* by Samuel Beckett, an Irishman who had been lecturing at the Sorbonne University for seven years and who was already acknowledged as an innovative novelist. He used minimal language. Through symbolism he showed basic human behaviour.

Shortly afterwards Eugene Ionesco's *The Bald Prima Donna*, followed by half a dozen other plays, gave rise to what was known as the 'Theatre of the Absurd'. Concurrently, Jean Genet, Albert Camus, Arrabal and others began an opposing cult – the 'Theatre of Cruelty'.

In Dunedin, at the other end of the world, Patric read these exciting new plays with delight, and John Griffin at the University Book Shop ensured their availability at the earliest possible moment. When our account with the bookshop got too big, he offset it with generous advertisements in programmes.

Waiting for Godot aroused a storm of derision in London in 1956, but when Patric read it he dubbed it great theatre and planned an immediate production. It so happened that the young critic dispatched to review the play had become a father the day the show opened, and he left in the interval. To give him his due, he had done his homework on Beckett but his comments on the second half of the play aired his knowledge of Beckett's *Endgame* instead of *Waiting for Godot*! Patric wrote to the editor requesting that his productions not be reviewed till the paper had a competent critic. It was almost a decade before another reviewer appeared on the scene.

Fortunately there were two daily papers at that time, and even the offending one had an arts page that continued to give us generous advance coverage regardless of how much, or little, we spent on advertising. But all publicity is valuable and we were now more dependent than ever on word-of-mouth and a high standard of production.

Our next venture into avant garde theatre was *The Maids* by Jean Genet. The complex roles of the maids themselves were played by Dallas Campbell and Beverley Knox. Even though they had had four or five years in our drama classes, they confessed later that the experience of being in the play blew their minds. Later, when the Globe Theatre was up and running, we did a second production. This time Dallas took the more mature role of Madame. She told me, 'If I had understood what I was saying in that first production I could never have given it such intensity of emotion – I would have been too embarrassed!'

Finding a home for *The Maids* was a headache, especially as it was guaranteed to draw small audiences. Patric tried every known location. Recalling my experience at the one-room Fireside Theatre in a Nottinghill Gate basement in London, and the work we had done at 84 London Street, I finally persuaded him to stage the play in our own drawing room – the 'big studio'. With the help of a local supporter, we went through the telephone book, compiled a mailing list, and issued invitations to the play with supper at £5 a head.

The response was marvellous numerically, but the reaction to Genet's text was exactly as expected. The fur-coat brigade fled, but the young and venturesome, particularly those who had come to our classes, were right behind us and their numbers were steadily increasing.

There was no way we would abandon them now.

CHAPTER III

Taking the Plunge

The Globe is built

੩ੈ

If the rest of New Zealand died on the weekends, Dunedin was in a state of *rigor mortis*. For the most part Patric and I were too busy to concern ourselves with entertainment but sometimes on a Saturday night we would treat ourselves to what we called a ceremonial dinner. There was always a good bottle of wine, and we would light candles and stage-manage the occasion in the finest style our ill-equipped house could afford. Patric would wear his velvet smoking jacket and flowered waistcoat, and I a long evening dress and perhaps even the beautiful velvet cloak edged with squirrel fur, which Patric had had made for me in Auckland from a Dior design. It continues to appear on the stage to this day. After dinner we would sit by an open fire, listen to music, read poetry to each other, or simply talk.

It was on such a night towards the end of 1960 that we began to take stock of our general situation. Since our severance with the Repertory Society, Rosalie and Patric Carey Productions had presented twenty-one plays in and around Dunedin, and perhaps the most satisfactory had been in our own house. Apart from the disastrous venture into the 'big time' at his Majesty's, which we were still paying off, we managed, by dint of extreme economy, to balance the budget on every show. Patric's costings were extraordinarily accurate, but we still depended on teaching and freelance work, generally outside Dunedin, for our livelihood.

Our biggest expenses were theatre hire, advertising, transport, and printing. For this reason, the drawing-room productions had many advantages. But even a large room had its problems. Apart from the limited space, there was only one entrance. When we did Ionesco's *The Chairs* the old people were required to make their exit through the window – great fun when it was raining or even snowing.

We were discussing our situation when Patric said, 'Why don't we build our own theatre?' Why not? We had a fine section near the city centre and it didn't seem to matter that we had less than no money, no car, no committee – and two small children to care for.

'I'll ring Niel Wales!' Patric said. Niel and his charming Tasmanian wife were great supporters of the arts but were also keen skiers and socialites, so were unlikely to be at home. As it happened Niel answered the telephone. His reaction was: 'It must be done!'

Next morning Patric was up early and off to town for a copy of the building regulations. As he breezed past me he called out, 'Ring Aubrey Stephens,' (our solicitor and keen supporter), 'and ask him to arrange a loan of £500.' During the ensuing weeks Patric wrote to all the local building suppliers asking for contributions of materials or for financial help. Aubrey drew a blank with the loan but charged us for phone calls we asked him not to make, and nothing else bore fruit. Most firms did not even bother to reply.

Undaunted we called a meeting of supporters and friends. The idea of building a theatre was received with enthusiasm. Niel Wales drew up the plans for a simple modern building but as one or two people lost confidence in the scheme, even that seemed beyond our reach. In a flippant mood I suggested that we could erect a marquee in the garden and use the best features of the two-tiered stages Patric had built for the productions in Burns Hall. It was 'back to the drawing board'.

While in Wellington, between engagements, Patric had spent time studying Elizabethan theatres, and had built a model of Shakespeare's Globe as far as it was understood at the time. After further discussion Niel obliged with a totally new design based on this concept. We pressed ahead for we firmly believed, as James K. Baxter put it in a little publication we produced in 1968:

> There are two elements which have to be joined together for the maintaining of a permanent and effective theatre centre in any New Zealand town. The first is the existence of a group of dedicated people with the dramatic experience, insight and intellectual calibre necessary to go on producing good plays while audiences fluctuate.

> The second necessary element is that there should be a place and a building where plays can be put on the stage. After experimenting in the production of plays by Greek, Jacobean and modern playwrights in halls, theatres churches and private gardens, Patric and Rosalie Carey decided first to make use of their own house at 104 London Street, Dunedin, and later – since these studio productions were satisfying both to the directors and the audiences – to build an actual theatre adjoining their house.

Above: Christopher Carey in garden of
104 London Street in 1959, with the
house in its original state.
Below: The house with completed Globe
Theatre attached.

Interior of Globe Theatre in 1961 viewed from tarras.

Above: Ern Joyce, Kevin White and Mervyn Jarvis in Waiting for Godot, *by Beckett, performed in the Burns Hall, 1959. (Friends of the Globe Theatre Collection, Hocken Library, Uare Taoka o Hakena, University of Otago, Dunedin.)*
Below: Shakespeare's Romeo and Juliet *in 1961 was the first production in the newly constructed Globe Theatre. Dallas Fairmaid played Juliet to Richard Butler's Romeo. Costumes were designed by Rodney Kennedy.*

Above: The foyer of the Globe Theatre, used for exhibitions, post-performance suppers and by Rosalie as a studio for drama classes. Clio observes from her purpose-built alcove.

Below: The lighting box overlooking the stage to the right of the auditorium. Actors would often sneak in to check the audience or watch the performance.

The city council gave us a permit for our theatre provided it was not a separate building but an 'extension to Mrs Carey's Studio'. This meant that our drawing room became the inner study in Shakespearean terms. It was no great loss, for the room was usually too damp and cold to teach in.

Above the centre section of the main stage was a tarras (or balcony) supported by two handsome pillars we had been given some time before. On either side, there were casement windows above, and doors below, with grilles for such scenes as the one in *Twelfth Night* where Malvolio is imprisoned.

Until such time as we could satisfy the fire regulations and provide the required number of toilets, we were obliged to operate as a private theatre. For many years actors and audience had to trail upstairs to our bathroom, where they were quite likely to find a couple of children in the bath, or use the outside free-standing toilet which was even further from the theatre. Nearby shrubs flourished or sulked according to their reaction to being watered by male members of the audience.

As a private theatre we were not allowed to advertise, and so were more dependent than ever on the goodwill of our members and the quality of our productions. As well, we were required to have the agreement of neighbours.

This job fell to me, but posed no great difficulty. There was some reluctance initially on the part of the late Misses Kaye, elderly ladies who lived in the colonial cottage next door. They rarely had visitors, but maintained a very beautiful garden which we looked out on from our upstairs windows. Apart from a polite nod, we had never previously communicated. Having been assured we would not be unruly or noisy, the elder Miss Kaye, whose grandfather I believe was the Mason's groom said, 'Oh well, my father used to say, "Remember, some people have to earn their living; we must be tolerant."'

There was one more major obstacle. Niel Wales' design had carefully avoided the destruction of a pohutukawa, but there was a big pear tree just where the building was to stand, and we were loath to cut it down. Towards the end of the summer holidays Fate stepped in and a great wind blew the pear tree to the ground.

The following weekend, on 31 January 1961, we began excavations for the theatre. Rudyard Kipling's line 'The glory of the garden occupieth all who come' could easily be adapted to the project. Actors, students, professional people, academics, housewives plus everyone we knew or who was known by someone else, were recruited to wield shovels, hammers, saws, or cart and pour concrete, often for the first time in their lives.

Our two children, then aged two-and-half and six, pushed seventy-two-pound concrete blocks in a little trolley down the bumpy path from the street to the back of the section. It was my job to supply morning and afternoon teas and 'dagwoods' for lunches. I also had to find excuses to telephone people and entice them to the working bees. All went well to begin with, but initial enthusiasm soon waned.

We relied on a good response at Easter, but not a soul came. Patric was deeply disappointed. However, about 11.30 a.m. on the Saturday, Peggy Stedman and three of her boys called to see us. Peggy was on her way home after a few days in hospital, and had her neck in a brace. Nothing daunted, she and her young family worked with us for most of the rest of the holiday.

The trouble with amateur labour is that architects' plans and building regulations can be quite abstruse, even for Patric, whose previous experience of carpentry had been confined to stage sets. When the retaining wall was three or four blocks high, a misinterpretation was discovered and we had to start all over again.

Miraculously we were able to enlist the support of Ben Elson, a qualified engineer, who had acted for us in the past. We had not seen him for a very long time but he was happy to help. Under his supervision the building proceeded steadily.

As the structure began to take shape Patric was reminded by the building inspector to urge Niel Wales to submit the plans – which Niel had been too busy to give him. He explained courteously that since our section immediately overlooked the municipal offices he could actually see what was going on and it was very difficult to show a blind eye.

In order to attach the new building to the old it was necessary to dismantle part of the bay window of the drawing room where the inner study was to be. It was at this stage that we did our most ambitious house production – Henrik Ibsen's *John Gabriel Borkman*, with Fred Kersh in the title role. Throughout one whole act John Gabriel is heard pacing back and forth in an upstairs room. Fortunately there were no wall-to-wall carpets in our house, as Fred did his pacing in our bedroom immediately above the stage. Fortunate too that I never attempted to go to bed before shows were over.

The third act of *John Gabriel Borkman* takes place on a snow-covered mountain. To create the desired effect Patric hung a canvas sky-cloth around the window bay, covered with black gauze, which, with clever lighting, created an amazing effect. Outside in the garden, he set up his sound and lighting controls under a tarpaulin. These he operated clad in overcoat, fur hat and gloves, for winter was setting in early.

On the last night there were no less than sixty people in the audience. A university professor who had been obliged to watch this long play sitting on a cushion on the floor, remarked afterwards, 'You Careys are amazing! I became so involved in the play that I even began to feel cold in the third act.'

'Not too surprising,' Patric informed him. 'It's snowing outside, and there's nothing between you and the elements but a piece of canvas.'

The opening date for the theatre was set for 31 May 1961. Patric was working full time on the construction, so our income depended entirely on my teaching. But it was all so exciting, watching the little building grow, that nothing else mattered. Almost every Saturday fourteen or fifteen helpers arrived. Some would be there all day. In the evening I would serve a two-course meal, the most popular and cheapest being a fore-quarter of second-grade mutton, roasted very slowly with water or fruit juice and a few herbs, served with plenty of vegetables. The sweet was generally jelly and homemade ice-cream. Afterwards work continued till supper time at 10 p.m.

The domed roof, which was Niel Wales' pride and joy, was constructed like a spider's web. Where the struts met in the centre, there is a hollow octagonal box into which we put programmes and messages for posterity. This enormous structure was built on the ground and later hoisted into place. How triumphant the team felt when it finally came to rest, settling comfortably on the supporting walls. (I watched it from the bedroom window having just come back from a few days in hospital.)

For economy of weight as well as money, the dome was covered in plywood and malthoid, ostensibly waterproofed by a covering of tar and sand, but it was far from satisfactory. Waterproofing became an ongoing saga at the Globe.

In an interview published in the *Listener* in 1973, Patric told O.E. Middleton:

I went to a dismantling firm and said, 'You're pulling down old houses. How cheaply can you sell me wood?' I think it was twenty-five shillings for a hundred feet of kauri. You got a crow-bar and you took out all the nails. And some of the wood was so hard that you couldn't even saw it with a bandsaw: we had to drill holes to get the nails in. We built the thing in three months … it seats seventy-six people. It was a pretty ramshackle place. Still at least it was a theatre; it had a thrust stage forty feet deep and twenty feet wide – eight hundred square feet. Just in materials we spent twelve thousand five hundred dollars.

When it came to ordering wood for the floor, there was none to be found, and time was becoming crucial. It so happened that my mother had come down from Auckland for a visit. She went to the woodyard, ordered the required amount of pine and paid the bill. Patric's embarrassment was such that he could hardly be civil but as it turned out my mother's gesture had saved the day. Even so we were hardpressed to be ready for the scheduled opening, and postponement was impossible as one of our cast had a prior commitment to be in another play.

We would have liked to have the whole building octagonal, but the shape of the available land prevented this. A small rectangular section projected behind the main area of the auditorium. Even with this, the seating capacity was only forty-five.

Our opening production was Shakespeare's *Romeo and Juliet,* with Dallas Campbell, our most experienced actress, as Juliet, and Richard Butler as Romeo. He was extremely handsome, played a guitar and sang well, but had never before acted in Shakespeare. About a fortnight before the opening night the splendid actress playing Juliet's Nurse had a heart attack, and could not face mounting the almost perpendicular ladder leading to the tarras for the bedroom and balcony scenes. I was familiar with most of the words, and was sorely tempted, but I knew that with wardrobe, publicity, and all my other duties, taking a part would be unthinkable, especially as Patric was already in the cast. I can see him now, at the dress rehearsal in his Old Capulet costume, calling out his lines from the top of a ladder while hanging lights in the auditorium.

Once again it was Peggy Stedman who came to the rescue. She not only made an excellent Nurse for Juliet, but realising that our Romeo was having difficulty with his words, took him to stay in her home for a week, fed him good food and his lines until he really knew them.

A few days later, our stalwart John Fairmaid, who was playing Mercutio with great aplomb, was obliged to withdraw owing to the death of his father. Michael Devine, a professional actor who was already rehearsing the next production, stepped into this most important role and gave a fine performance.

Another young man who had been a tower of strength during building operations, and who was playing a couple of tiny parts which fortunately could be taken over by the 'extras', failed to appear at the dress rehearsal, and we have never seen or heard of him since.

About four o'clock on the opening day, we realised to our horror that there were no steps up to the theatre entrance, which was over a metre above ground. How was the audience to get in? A tired building crew – mostly the cast – undertook this final hurdle of making a set of steps. A tiny foyer was yet to be built, so in the meantime a small table was set up in the aisle just inside the door, adding to the difficulty of packing the people in. Inevitably the show opened a little late, but ran without further noticeable hitch.

I saw the play from the back of the auditorium where I stood peering over the heads of others. But like everyone else I was enchanted to hear Shakespeare's words spoken 'trippingly on the tongue', with naturalistic gestures, uncluttered by elaborate scenery. Curtains below the tarras allowed for changes of furniture and the play flowed along as it was meant to do. (It has been fascinating reading the enthusiastic reaction of critics to performances in the reconstructed Globe in London in the 1990s and to note that Dunedin audiences made this discovery over thirty years before.)

For *Romeo and Juliet* Rodney Kennedy was in charge of the wardrobe. We always enjoyed having Rodney involved. On one occasion when Patric and I were still sleeping in the 'little studio', I was in bed with a severe dose of flu when Rodney, who was under five feet tall, came up the path buried under a pile of costumes and fabrics. He spread them out on the floor of the studio along with all the donated materials and garments. Having discarded all incompatible colours he proceeded to put into piles everything that could be used for each character. He did a rough sketch and left me to see it come to fruition as best I could. Then at the end of a long arduous afternoon Rodney sent us into fits of laughter – and coughing – by standing on a stool, waggling his hips hula-style, dressed in a very long garment that came well below his feet.

Hats and appropriate coiffures were most important to Rodney and to me, no costume being considered complete without them. Shoes too are very significant and I could not stess strongly enough the importance of actors rehearsing in appropriate footwear.

Thanks to Rodney's impeccable eye for colour and the resources of Norman McKinlay's shoe and hat factory allied with donated fabrics, the costumes were truly beautiful. I shall never forget the effect of the dancers through the arch under the tarras lit by flickering firelight in the absence of adequate artificial light and the sheer beauty of Dallas lying on the bier under the tarras, with soft light on her long fair hair, and her pink and silver gown.

Coincidentally, *Romeo and Juliet* was also the choice of the New Zealand Players. Richard Campion, in all good faith, wrote to us suggesting we should choose another play as he was bringing his production to Dunedin. Fortunately we went ahead with our plans, for it transpired that his tour ended prematurely, whereas we were more than sold out before we opened. David Carnegie, author of *The Carey Years: Australasian Drama Studies*, quotes this observation made by one of the audience:

> I will merely say that this charming little theatre does look like any picture I have seen of London's former Globe ... It was delightful to see a Shakespearean production in the type of theatre for which it had originally been written, and if those in the front seats felt imperilled when the rapiers were flashing, at least they could feel themselves part of the performance!

Hopefully the audience did not see everything, such as the moment when Romeo (who was particularly athletic) scaled up a pillar to join Juliet on the balcony. On the first night he remained poised halfway up for an unduly long time. A wry smile crept over Juliet's face. A lesser actress would have 'corpsed' as we say in the theatre. Romeo's tights had caught on a nail in a very awkward place!

Our second production, Samuel Beckett's *Endgame*, opened to about fifteen people. The second night we played to two.

CHAPTER IV

Upstream

Plays – Drama classes – Exhibitions

❧

When I saw *Endgame* on the first night I could not make head nor tail of it. Beckett claims his words mean exactly what they say, and on the second night I found this to be absolutely true, apart from one line that haunts me still: 'There are no more bicycle wheels.'

On the surface Beckett reduces language to its bare essentials, but every phrase is loaded with underlying meaning. Of the four characters in *Endgame* one is a blind hypochondriac, one a dreamer who can see what is beyond but who never does anything, and the two old people who have been relegated to dustbins. We found this very funny at the time, having yet to learn that this was the fate of all too many of the elderly.

Patric was philosophical about the small audiences which were, he claimed, only to be expected, but we could ill afford a set-back to our finances. We sat down and reviewed the situation. Our biggest expenses now were royalties and printing. There was nothing much we could do about royalties apart from our established policy of endeavouring to balance new plays with old. It also helped that being professionals we were often able to do plays unavailable to amateurs and were given better rates.

For Saroyan's *The Cave Dwellers*, which we had staged in the university's Allen Hall, I duly applied to the three New Zealand agents, none of whom held the rights. I wrote to the publishers who sent me an address for Saroyan's agent. I wrote to him in New York, but he no longer represented Mr Saroyan who now lived in Switzerland. There was no reply to the letter I sent care of the agent. We certainly made no objections if no one wanted our money.

Printing of programmes was a major expense so, as if he had not enough to do already (outside productions and adjudicating Theatre Federation festivals still being a major part of his income), Patric bought a small printing press. One of Peggy Stedman's sons, a master printer, helped Patric get started. Handsetting is a slow painstaking job that could not be farmed out easily, and before long it took its toll on Patric's eyesight. He bought himself a pair of glasses from Woolworth's and eventually we acquired a broken-down Gestetner duplicator, which meant we could handset the covers while the general information could be loose-leaf – usually done by me on an elderly portable typewriter. The ancient duplicator required two turns of the handle for every sheet but it soldiered on even when our membership exceeded five hundred.

Having a theatre to work in was a great stimulus to my studio teaching, even though preparations for the next set frequently meant the stage was in chaos when I wanted to work there. Many classes began with a 'hands on' operation clearing a space.

Students were responding well to the idea of creative drama and the intermediate class evolved an incredibly clever improvisation – *A Beatnik for Christmas* – which developed into a play. Typical of that time it was not set in New Zealand, but in an artist's basement flat in London. One of their number (Kristin Chance) had been reading about the beat cult and undertook to script the play in appropriate language. We entered our effort in the local drama festival to the utter bewilderment of the adjudicator, who nevertheless awarded us second place.

One of the characters spent most of the performance upside down flaunting blue feet. The young man in question was Michael Guest, later to become a barrister, broadcaster, city councillor and Family Court judge. Many years later when I needed some legal advice, Michael greeted me warmly and said, 'I'd be happy if I can say thank you in some way for the confidence you have given me in my professional career.' When he knew I was writing this book he volunteered the following:

> I have the fondest memories of the Globe Theatre and Rosalie and Patric Carey. For over twenty-five years of my life from the age of three I lived just across the road at 93 London Street and trips to the Globe were a regular part of my life.

> In the rather repressive years of the late fifties and early sixties in New Zealand, it was rather 'odd' to have neighbours who lived for art. There was always something new on at the Globe and as a very young schoolboy it appeared to me that what the theatre presented abounded with variety.

> There was comedy, tragedy, melodrama, beautifully costumed drama and *Hamlet* in modern dress. There were successful productions of quasi-

musicals and all manner of theatrical delights which thoroughly enriched Dunedin and proved that the city had a theatrical intellect a little above the annual staging of the Miss New Zealand Show ...

But it was the personalities of Rosalie and Patric which, to me, made the concept and reality of the theatre so vibrant ...

I can vividly recall Rosalie and Patric both acting and directing. When Patric acted – in the few small parts that I observed – he was normally cast in the rather dark and sombre role, not unlike a James K. Baxter figure, and I found his persona as an actor rather forbidding. However, when he took over the role of director, his ability to communicate mood and feeling and atmosphere was second to none, and it was rather thrilling as a young stagehand to gain a real feeling for what directing was all about.

When Rosalie directed the younger budding actors of the time, she was more given to passion and expression in extracting the best from them, but my unforgettable memory of her – apart from her laugh at the post-production parties – was her ability to act. More than twenty years on, my mind's eye clearly contains the picture on occasion after occasion of Rosalie lighting up the stage, with her exercising that Carey concentration and control when centre stage, back stage, on the balcony or wherever. She was a gem.

The studio was not only a training ground – for adults as well as children – it was also a splendid source of personnel for the plays. Patric would sit up in the lighting box and watch classes in action, then swoop like an eagle on its prey when he saw the talent he wanted.

Working bees were another source of new blood. Dallas Campbell was not only a willing helper herself, but she also brought several new recruits. In our anniversary booklet *The Globe Theatre – a Celebration of 25 Years, 1961–86*, Graeme Smith tells his experience:

'If you help with the working bee on Saturday you can go to the party on Saturday night.'

Not very auspicious words in themselves but that is just how I began my association with the Globe Theatre. In those days I hadn't a clue what 'The Theatre' meant, but I helped at the working bee and I went to the party and I've been there ever since. Actually the association began a couple of weeks after the party when I met Dallas Fairmaid (Campbell in those days) in George Street and she told me that 'Rosalie wants to see you.' 'Rosalie who?' 'Rosalie Carey, she wants you to help with a play.'

That was what started it all, and it was a Greek play to boot. I soon learned that 'The Theatre' wasn't as airy fairy as most people thought, particularly when the general populace of Dunedin had been subjected to Patric in his 'Sherlock Holmes' overcoat and goatee after he arrived from England as the producer for the Repertory Society. When I came in contact with Patric the goatee had spread sideways and upwards more or less as it is today.

I started backstage and that's where I stayed with only the odd step into the lights when it couldn't be avoided such as the time Patric handed me a script and said 'I've got a part for you in this play.' Well, I read the script and found the part with the least amount of dialogue and presented myself for the reading. I was quite stunned to find that the character Patric had picked for me was one of the biggest parts. My reaction was to tell him 'You've got to be out of your mind, I can't do a part like that, it's too much for me to learn.' ... Patric pulled one of his famous 'If I didn't think you could do it, I wouldn't have asked you' trips (you've really no way out of that one).

Another of Dallas's finds was an American whom we knew as 'Tigger'. She was an unusual girl and Patric immediately saw her as an ideal Laura, the lame daughter in Tennessee Williams' *The Glass Menagerie.* Pamela Pow, who later performed both for the Fortune Theatre in Dunedin and the Court in Christchurch, played Amanda, the mother, with the flair she brought to every role she undertook. David Mitchell (now David Warbeck, actor and model in London) as her son won the hearts of the St Hilda's girls who came to the show 'en masse' and queued up for his autograph. Years later Fred Kersh reminisced 'That long speech when David leaned against the wall with the lights flickering from the adjacent dance-hall was so moving I couldn't believe I was watching a play.'

My first professional engagement in England (with the Adelphi Guild Theatre) had ended prematurely as a result of a cut in Arts Council funding to provincial companies in order to support a major West End production. Since it starred Vivienne Leigh and Marlon Brando we naturally thought such a show should be self-supporting. A particular disappointment for me was that I should miss the opportunity of working with Maurice Browne, a highly respected American director engaged for the forthcoming production of Ibsen's *Hedda Gabler.* I loved the play and so stayed with the company for an extra week at my own expense, to see the first night and lend a helping hand.

So it was a great day for me when fifteen years later, towards the end of 1961, Patric gave me the opportunity to play the coveted role of Hedda. In the cast were Fred Kersh, Keith Harrison, Natalie Ellis and Irene Adcock, who was living in Dunedin to be with her daughter Fleur and young grandson Andrew. I was concerned that I might have too much to cope with if required to make my usual contribution to designing and organising the wardrobe. Irene Adcock offered to help and then one of my adult pupils asked if I would 'allow' her to make my costumes. I was delighted and they were beautiful.

Well into rehearsals we were still without an Eyelot Lovborg and I had one of my most important scenes with him. In the nick of time a friend of Irene's, John O'Leary, arrived from Auckland and took the part. Inadequate rehearsal made me very nervous, but many years later O.E. Middleton wrote warmly of my performance. What I really looked forward to was rehearsing the wonderful scene at the end of Act III when Hedda tears up Lovborg's manuscript and thrusts it into the stove exclaiming, 'I am burning your child!' When the great moment came at rehearsal Patric announced, 'Ten o'clock. Time for tea!' Deflated, I performed the scene for 'Mrs Seats' and 'Mr Floor', unseen by anyone until the dress rehearsal.

After the season Patric gave an Edwardian dinner in the theatre for the cast and helpers. He created a refectory table out of two doors on trestles, and set it up beautifully with white linen tablecloths, candles and flowers. We all wore appropriate costume and behaved with fitting gentility – at least as far as I was aware.

Recently Natalie Ellis reminisced:

It was a wonderful night. For one of the various courses Patric served mushrooms – big black ones. After eating them we noticed that all our teeth were black, which we found very funny. Oh yes! And I hadn't fixed my hair-piece properly, and it fell into the soup!

Bernard Shaw's *Arms and the Man* is one of my favourite plays. It has wonderful characters, neat twists to the story, and an abundance of laughs. As a teenager I heard it read by a team of very competent actors and while with the Adelphis I understudied the leading role. Inevitably when Patric decided to direct it in 1962 I longed to play Catherine, the mother, but I was slowly coming to grips with the fact that unless another miracle happened, my time must be spent elsewhere, especially for costume plays.

I designed and oversaw the making of hundreds of costumes but always made a point of having an assistant as official wardrobe mistress, and this time Irene Adcock was a tower of strength.

Arms and the Man benefited greatly from having the two-tiered stage, it being one of the few occasions when Bluntschli's ascent up the drainpipe to Raina's bedroom could actually be seen. It was altogether a highly successful production and on the Sunday following the final performance John Fairmaid and Dallas Campbell, the romantic leads in the play if not off-stage as well, arrived at ten in the morning to help clean up the theatre. This was typical of the special attitude developing among members which enabled the theatre to succeed.

Oliver Goldsmith's *She Stoops to Conquer* is also a 'must' for any self-respecting programme, if one has the cast and the costumes. In our first production of this entertaining classic, in 1962, Dallas once again took the lead, this time opposite Michael Shackleton, a surgeon whose rehearsal time was frequently interrupted by calls from the hospital.

Our costumes for this production were remarkably beautiful especially considering that I was given no official allocation of money. All the materials were donated – most of them being silks and brocades given to CORSO and of no possible use to them. Moira Fleming, enthusiastic, multi-talented President of the Friends, was a tower of strength, helping with the wardrobe, hairdressing, and publicity. A great team of helpers carried out my badly sketched designs with remarkable ingenuity. Furthermore we had beautiful nylon wigs sent to us by Anne de Roo, who was then in England.

But life cannot be rosy all the way. In the midst of rehearsals for *She Stoops to Conquer* Patric went out of town leaving me to hold the reins. Unfortunately I developed a severe dose of flu and could hardly hold my head up. There was no choice though, but to attend rehearsals and to continue encouraging my sewing team.

One night as I sat in the stalls with my head and back aching, I lost the battle and drifted into sleep. Later one of the cast remarked, 'You're a rotten producer. You go to sleep in rehearsals!'

In order to keep the momentum going and be one leap ahead of our creditors it was necessary to maintain a ridiculously ambitious programme. Therefore we were very grateful for two guest productions – Spewack's *Under the Sycamore Tree*, and Graham Greene's *The Potting Shed*, directed by Pamela Pow and Mary Middleditch respectively.

By 1962 Dunedin's theatrical reputation was growing fast, and could well be compared with Wellington's. In the capital, the Repertory Society had employed professional directors (Patric included) for some years, and Unity Theatre flourished under the capable direction of Nola Millar. Whereas audiences there allowed for a run of one or two weeks, the normal season in Dunedin was only four nights. However, having no rent to pay we could introduce a season of ten performances – two weekends plus Tuesday, Wednesday, and Thursday – which gave casts the benefit of extra experience, and two Saturday night parties.

By the end of the first year at the Globe, three thousand people had seen seventy-one performances of fourteen plays ranging from Shakespeare to Beckett. The theatre had cost £15,000 for materials, much of which had been paid off. In the programme for Ibsen's *Little Eyolf* there was a plea to:

> make a final effort to raise the remaining £750 which will enable us to pay off the bank loans and complete the building, including the sixteen-foot extension which our rapidly increasing audience makes essential.

The Southern Comedy Players were also flourishing. In spite of long distances between venues, inclement weather and largely uninitiated audiences they had made eight tours of the South Island and one of the North. However David Carnegie, who had come from Canada and Britain not long before, wrote:

> Although this company has now been operating for some years on a professional basis one cannot escape the impression that it is composed very largely of talented amateurs, who have acquired a superficial slickness through continuity of playing…

Possibly because of Patric's and my background, and the standard we achieved, our little theatre was always looked upon as professional even though no one, including ourselves, was actually paid a salary. Much later I learnt that for many years actors at Downstage, too, retained their regular jobs and received no more than £4 a week.

The irony of the amateur/professional situation was highlighted when Jonathan Hardy, actor, filmscript writer, and for some years director of Auckland's Mercury Theatre, returned from a tour with the Southern Comedy Players and asked Patric if he could work with us, as he wanted to claim that he had been performing at the Globe and not solely with the Southern Comedy Players. The vehicle for Jonathan's talents was the two-hander *The New Tenant* by Eugene Ionesco in which he gave a fine performance well matched by Peggy Durrant, a stalwart of our theatre, as the landlady.

Patric became very enthusiastic about the new wave theatre, his next choice being *The Stranger* by Albert Camus, who was little known as a dramatist but whose novels had delighted him. Patric had a problem deciding upon a leading man, but eventually contacted August Varvosovsky, a wonderful character who had been an opera singer in Vienna till he was sent by the Nazis to work in the salt mines of Silesia. Since coming to Dunedin he had worked in the bakery managed by Mary Middleditch, who was a successful business woman as well as a talented producer.

August had earlier given fine performances for us in *The Cave Dwellers* (Saroyan) and in the title role of *Don Bludgeon was a Puppet* by Garcia Lorca. However, after two or three rehearsals of *The Stranger* August came to Patric in great distress. He was having major problems in his private life and felt it was unfair to continue with the role. Years later he expressed extreme gratitude for Patric's understanding. He was also full of praise for him as a director. He told me, '…Patric allowed people to discover parts of themselves they were unaware of.'

For the role in *The Stranger* Patric rang Keith Harrison. Although we had not seen him or his talented wife Patricia for quite some time, Keith came to the rescue without hesitation and gave his usual dynamic performance. As we sat down to our evening meal on the first night I remarked to Patric, 'There must be something wrong. Here we are on the opening night of a new play, sitting peacefully at dinner and everything is under control.'

To round off the Globe's second year we decided to let our hair down with our own adaptation of the famous melodrama *Maria Marten*. Patric had directed it most successfully for both Wellington and Dunedin repertory societies and we were able to have Moira Fleming and Betty Dodds, both of whom had given wonderful performances in Dunedin's Opera House, as Maria and Mrs Marten.

We had no piano (I used to play reasonably well in my youth and was sad to be without one), so I had bought an old harmonium for all of £5. This was ideal for the show, especially when played by as entertaining a pianist as Pam Dawber. Audiences disappointed numerically, but those who did come remember it with delight, especially the traditional throwing of objects onto the stage.

As usual we had guest artists to entertain between acts. Beverley Pollock, broadcaster, journalist, and beautiful actress and singer was memorable in her rendering of 'She was Poor but She was Honest'. Audiences responded with a shower of pennies that our children gathered with glee after each performance. Small cabbages and sticks of rhubarb were bounty for us. Every bit was gathered and served on the Careys' table. A further bonus for me was that I was able to tread the boards in a wonderfully different capacity.

Betty Dodds and I sang an 'out-of-tune' duet. Betty, who was comfortably plump, was resplendent in pink satin brocade; while I, who was more than usually thin at the time, wore a beautiful mauve, lime and silver gown adapted from my favourite evening dress. Betty had a fine contralto voice while I sang soprano – except when we switched parts as an extra gimmick. At the dress rehearsal Belinda (aged three-and-a-half) wandered onto the stage and remained clutching her mother's skirts for the rest of the item. It caused considerable amusement so Patric said, 'Keep it in.'

At one performance Betty and I thought we were a particular hit, for the laughter was much greater than usual. Later we learned that Belinda had stolen the show by innocently picking her nose!

Summer productions gave us more work than income but our exhibitions of paintings and pottery, which included work by Doreen Blumhardt, Len Castle, and Barry Brickell, put the Globe on the map as being much more than simply a playhouse.

In the autumn, we had so much enjoyment from our production of Aristophanes' ever-green satirical comedy, *Lysistrata*, its anti-war theme being particularly dear to our hearts, that even a poor box office would not have mattered. We had assembled a strong cast headed by Dallas Campbell but needed an imposing figure to play the Magistrate, who has a hilarious scene with his wife. Myrrhine (Karen Reid), carries out Lysistrata's edict that women should not sleep with their men, no matter what lengths they may go to, until the men agree to give up fighting wars.

As so often happened the right actor was found purely by chance. After every performance we served free coffee and biscuits for audience and cast, to encourage socialising and discussion of the plays, many of which were complex and controversial. It was on such an occasion that I 'rediscovered' Paul Armfelt. He had come to see our production of Sartre's *Huis Clos* because a friend was in the cast. I first met Paul in Cornwall back in the forties when he was a mining student. We both appeared in Dodie Smith's *Dear Octopus* at the little Studio Theatre in Cambourne. Paul often quotes his favourite line spoken by one of the children in the play: 'I know a dirty word – District Nurse!'

How innocent children were (and adults too, for that matter), in the 'good old days'! Even in our time, Paul recalls that at rehearsals for *Lysistrata* Dallas could not bring herself to say the word 'breast'. Dallas laughs now about this naivety, recognising how much she, and many others, grew up in the stimulating atmosphere of the Globe, which for many people was becoming the cultural hub of Dunedin.

THE GLOBE THEATRE.

Under the Direction of Mr. & Mrs. Carey.

MARIA MARTEN; ———— OVERWHELMING SUCCESS !!!

Every anticipation which the Proprietors had formed is now most fully and unequivocally realized; and MARIA MARTEN stands confessed the most successful Drama of the Season. The breath -less anxiety which each scene was listened to - and the pain- full interest it excited in every bosom, can alone be equalled by that deafening applause of the fashionable audience.

MARIA MARTEN

or,

MURDER in the RED BARN

the true & tragic history

of the late lamentable crime

in the county of Sussex.

Containing

an appalling MORAL warning

to wantons.

Not an order will be admitted, & free list suspended.

VIVAT REGINA

Hand-set notice for Maria Marten, *1962*

Above: In Good King Charles's Golden Days *by Bernard Shaw. Left to right: Robin Patterson, Eric Herd, Barbara Manton and Rosalie Carey, 1964.*
Below: 1964 production of The Night of the Iguana, *by Tennessee Williams. Left to right: Bert Nesbit, Gay McInnes and Michael Noonan.*

Above left: Rosalie in Ibsen's Hedda Gabler, *1961.*
Above right: Pat Harrison and Christopher Carey in Little Eyolf, *by Ibsen, 1962.*
Below: Patric Carey in the theatre foyer with artworks during one of the many exhibitions held at the Globe.

CHAPTER V

Exploring New Ground

Wesker … Ibsen … Chekhov …

ᔫ

England's most significant new dramatist since John Osborne of *Look Back in Anger* fame was a cockney Jew – Arnold Wesker. As well as peopling his plays from the working class, not often seen on the London stage, Wesker blazed something of a trail by writing a trilogy. Patric felt this young man had a great future. There have been many productions since, particularly of the second play *Roots*, but we were certainly the first and probably the only theatre in New Zealand to do all three, especially in one year – 1963.

Chronologically the trilogy began with *Chicken Soup with Barley* but *Roots*, the second play, was the first to see the light in London. As it happened, it was more convenient for us to schedule Patric's production of *Chicken Soup with Barley* a little later. The Globe production of *Roots* was directed by Pamela Pow with Natalie Ellis in the leading role. Natalie had worked with us first as a pupil and then in many plays before and after the theatre was built. She has also continued to perform in and produce a host of plays for the Repertory Society and Fortune Theatre, to say nothing of directing and teaching at Columba College. She is still making a major contribution to theatre.

One night during rehearsals for *Roots* Natalie arrived very late – unheard of for her. It transpired that she had been in a motor accident. Her nose was broken, and her face badly bruised so the show was postponed for some weeks. There were other plays in between but the trilogy was done in sequence after all.

Chicken Soup with Barley, which I regard as little more than a rewrite of Sean O'Casey's *Juno and the Paycock,* was dogged with misfortune. One character had a drinking problem, another was in trouble with the police, but it was a case of 'the show must go on' and of course it did, though it hardly emerged triumphant.

I directed *I'm Talking about Jerusalem* with no memorable problems. I had a very good cast which included Heather Douglas, a stalwart of the Phoenix Players, and our son Christopher in his second speaking part, his first having been in Ibsen's *Little Eyolf.*

Dunedin was becoming more theatre-minded but we were still struggling to make ends meet even though we were averaging ten or twelve productions a year. Meanwhile the Repertory Society was flourishing, the Phoenix Players performed intermittently but well, and OUDS (the Otago University Drama Society) was doing some excellent work under the skilled guidance of Rodney Kennedy. They even had two original one-act plays to their credit, *The Rattle* by Michael Noonan (later Michael Antony Noonan) and *Conversations with a Golliwog* by Alex Guyan. The latter play was a wonderful idea but needed a lot of editing, which came later.

The night we saw it, Patric and I were sitting in front of John McIndoe, the publisher. Patric turned to him and said, 'Why don't you publish these plays? Drama festivals are crying out for new one-act plays and there are practically no locally written ones.'

John accepted the challenge and *Conversations with a Golliwog* became one of the most frequently performed plays in festivals throughout New Zealand.

At the time, William Austin was head of radio drama, and always keen to nurture indigenous writing. He commissioned Alex and Michael to write plays for radio. This was how Alex came to write *Modern Man at Breakfast* but I'm not aware of his having written anything else of significance. Michael Noonan, on the other hand, wrote extensively for radio and television and was joint scriptwriter for the TV series *The Governor.*

Although a number of my younger students were becoming competent actors, it was still difficult to cast a juvenile lead, as we found when producing Turgenev's beautiful slow-moving play *A Month in the Country* early in 1963. But later that same year, when Mary Middleditch directed Han Hsuing's delightful *Lady Precious Stream,* she cast fifteen-year-old Gabrielle Johnston (alternating with Pauline Young) in the title role, and had several other of my bright young people in the very large cast, most of whom were experienced actors from the Phoenix Players.

This charming play, based on a Chinese folk tale and written in the formal style of Chinese theatre, is eminently suitable for children. Visually it was magnificent. All the royal characters disported themselves in genuine pre-revolution Chinese court costumes from the inner portals of the Otago Museum and Mary ensured that all others looked sartorially comparable. It was rare for us to have a play that could be enjoyed by whole families and they came in droves. At the matinée children were sitting on the stage, in the aisles and on their parents' laps. What the fire chief would have said I hate to think.

Patric's Chekhov productions were a special feature at the Globe, the first being *The Cherry Orchard* with Barbara Manton and Fred Kersh in the leading roles. Playing dates coincided with Easter, so we decided upon four nights before the holiday and four the following week. A Russian trade legation was in Dunedin at the time, and one of our patrons, Nicholas Zisserman, who taught Russian at the university, asked if he could bring them to the theatre. They had missed the first season and were leaving on the day we began the second. We had already decided to have a rehearsal on the Tuesday night so we made it a dress rehearsal and invited them. They all sat in the front row with Nicholas, who gave a running commentary in a loud voice, in Russian, throughout the play. What a challenge to the actors' concentration! At least this was a rehearsal, but on another occasion Nicholas brought his elderly mother to a Chekhov production and did the same thing for her.

Ibsen was also very important in the Globe calendar – particularly the late plays, which are rarely performed. To our great delight we were invited to take our production of *Rosmersholm* to Christchurch. By this time we were – justifiably, I believe – proud of our standards and looked forward to performing for a larger audience. It was a great treat for all of us to have a weekend away. We stayed at one of the better known hotels. Alas, we found the service disappointing, to say the least. The local organisation was also less than we had hoped. No furniture or properties were ready when we arrived, and apart from one very good press article, publicity was almost non-existent.

Although we had been told we should be playing in the new Ngaio Marsh Theatre, we found ourselves booked into the lecture theatre of the museum. Paul Armfelt, who played Rosmer opposite Beverley Pollock as Rebecca West, had this to say:

> Imagine our shock, horror and dismay when we discovered that all our entrances had to be made in full view of the audiences. There were no wings nor any provision for a prompt – Betty Ussher had the job as I recall – so we had to trust to our good memories and other wiles to get through two performances … but we managed.

One of the company was unable to travel with us and the only rehearsal possible for his replacement was in the car driving to Christchurch. In spite of all these difficulties the critique in the Christchurch *Press* was headed: 'IBSEN'S ROSMERSHOLM REWARDING EXPERIENCE'. The report went on to say:

> It is a long time since Ibsen has been played on a Christchurch stage. It says little for theatre groups here that it should be left to a visiting company – Dunedin's noted Globe Theatre of Patric and Rosalie Carey – to rectify this neglect. This company last night presented a compelling *Rosmersholm* in the museum theatre ... Here were characterisations clearly defined and unwaveringly developed. Awareness of acting diminished rapidly as these characters grew in life.
>
> DEVOTED
>
> The effect was such that, though the cast cannot be described strictly as professional (except for Patric Carey) one would happily bundle it into a vehicle and take it on tour anywhere and everywhere. Here was that rewarding experience of people devoted to theatre expressing its art to a wonderful degree. There were none of the elements of those actors who merely enjoy theatre. The overall impression was that of vocation instead – in brief, theatre.
>
> CONTROLLED
>
> There was no jarring note. The play's tragic mood was clearly established and allowed to develop unencumbered. The production was given with such controlled intensity that Ibsen's economy in dialogue showed up particularly well and even the briefest of remarks gained the intensity the dramatist intended ...

It seemed as if we had arrived at last! Not only was it a rave notice but here was a critic who appreciated precisely what Patric set out to do – to discover and portray the dramatist's intention. The review was published on 22 November 1963 – the day President John F. Kennedy was assassinated – and Christchurch, like most of the rest of the world, was plunged into deep gloom. Even those who did come to the theatre, including ourselves, were in no mood to be entertained.

On the Sunday, a coffee morning was arranged at which Patric and I performed *Fando and Lis,* a two-hander – part of a double-bill with *Orisons* by contemporary writer Arrabal of the Theatre of Cruelty. Again attendances disappointed, but we were honoured by a brief visit from Ngaio Marsh, the great detective story writer, who had so much influence on theatre in Christchurch in the forties. Much later, quite unsolicited, she called to see us in Dunedin. Contrary to expectations I found her very easy to talk to, but regretted that Patric was not home, for I believe theirs would have been a 'marriage of true minds'. As directors both had the utmost respect for the playwright's intention, and believed that every production was an exciting tour of exploration seeking out hidden depths in the actors and the author.

We were full of optimism. Our local audiences were growing and we were being recognised not only in other centres but also for other reasons. Because of Patric's propensity to favour the work of such dramatists as Ibsen, Chekhov, and Strindberg, with their deep psychological insight and use of symbolism, psychiatrists brought their patients to the plays in order to assess their reactions. University lecturers encouraged science and medical students to broaden their horizons by coming to the theatre, and many careers changed course as a consequence of this association with the Globe.

For instance, at one after-show party, I found myself talking to a young man who had been brought by a member of the cast to be cheered up because he was suffering from a broken romance. I suggested that the best cure for his problem was to be in a play. He liked the idea and we cast him as one of the young officers in *The Cherry Orchard*. It was a small part. He had little acting experience, but was a personable young man and we recognised his potential. Very shortly afterwards, Patric gave him the demanding lead in Gogol's *The Government Inspector*. He was a joy to work with and he was more than pleased to be involved in the arts. He had been unhappy not only in his love-life but also at the university. Rather than be a pale shadow of his older brother, who was a lecturer in English, Christopher Thompson had chosen to major in the sciences. Encouraged by Patric, he applied for a job in television where he became a successful director, first in New Zealand and later, even more so, in Australia and the United States.

The cast of *The Government Inspector* involves only five women but twenty men, though fortunately some parts can be doubled. Nevertheless it was not easy to find such a number, especially towards the end of the academic year. So we had Lance Tonkin, who dreamed of playing Macbeth, but was well past his prime, and exercised to learn a very small part; and we had Nicholas Zisserman. End of term was no particular bother to Nicholas since, as he said, 'I have only three and a half students.' (The 'half' was part-time.)

Nicholas was a White Russian who had spent some years in China before coming to New Zealand and was quite a character. He had a large ferocious-looking dog he was convinced would never hurt anyone. That may have been so, but it had a disconcerting habit of pouncing on people as they came up the path to the theatre, to their extreme alarm. When one of its victims tried to order it off, Nicholas shouted, 'It is no use to talk to him like that, he only speaks Russian!' On one occasion he stood in the garden and called out to the upstairs dressing room, 'Is Mrs Fairmaid in the play? I only come when Mrs Fairmaid is in the play.'

While playing in *The Government Inspector*, Nicholas came to the theatre each evening with Lance Tonkin, who drove a car that looked as antiquated as himself. Contrary to normal Globe practices, these two regularly arrived at the theatre already dressed in their stage costumes – frock coats, stiff collars, and top hats. One evening, they were involved in a slight motor accident at the crossroads at the foot of the London Street hill. Inevitably traffic officers and police appeared forbidding them to leave the scene. One of our friends passing at the time was highly entertained to see these two august gentlemen protesting to the officials in loud voices, with much waving of arms, 'But we are in the play!'

The university modern languages department did an annual production at the Globe, in French or German in alternate years. That year the Russian department had a turn, with an abridged version of *The Government Inspector* using our set and costumes and, to a large extent, our audience as well. Inevitably Nicholas was in the cast. This was the highlight of his career – to be in a favourite play, and in Russian!

CHAPTER VI

Offshoots

Downstage – Central Theatre – Little Dolphin – Gateway

ॐ

It was not only in Dunedin that theatre was taking new and inspired directions. In Wellington four actors – Tim Elliott, Peter Bland, Martyn Sanderson, and Harry Seresin – and their wives felt it was time to establish professional theatre in the capital. As they said, 'If the Careys can do it, why can't we?' Why not indeed? After all they had a pool of actors with vast experience with Repertory and Unity theatres, and had had professional directors, some from overseas, since the early fifties.

Tim Elliott came to see us. Patric could spare only an hour or two, but it was holiday time and I spent a whole day answering questions and sharing what expertise and experience I could offer. In 1964 the quartet opened a restaurant theatre in a cramped upstairs space in Courtenay Place, the site of the present Downstage, largely thanks to a handsome initial gift of £150,000 from Sheilah Winn and the Hannah Trust. Later this rose to $360,000.

In Auckland Mary Amoore founded Central Theatre in a disused garage in Remuera and has readily attributed its inspiration to the Globe. There was also the shortlived Little Dolphin Theatre in Hawera founded by Peter Trim who had been a patron of ours; and later, in Tauranga, Peter Tulloch and his wife, Maureen Edwards, established the Gateway Theatre. Peter had worked in Dunedin at the Playhouse, and Maureen had been a pupil, teacher and favourite actress at the Globe. The Gateway flourished for several years till the couple went to work on stage and screen in Australia.

In 1964 we were still paying off debts and though Paul Armfelt, who had become an architect, had drawn up the plans for an extension to our auditorium and foyer, we did not feel sufficiently secure financially to undertake this ambitious programme.

It was a huge challenge competing with the Southern Players, who had an influential board of governors and Arts Council funding. They had been able to acquire and redecorate the Playhouse most attractively, and install comfortable seats – very different from our hard wooden ones. Furthermore, they were near a bus route – one stop from the bottom of London Street – while we were very near the top.

Needless to say no help for us was forthcoming from the Arts Council. Whereas after long experience Patric and I firmly believed that a permanent home was essential for good quality theatre, it had been their policy not to contribute to capital improvements. They compromised by giving us £200 a year for royalities.

Obviously we had not learnt the technique of acquiring funds. Patric always sustained a wonderful rapport with his casts (generally speaking they 'loved the man this side of idolatry') but he was too much of an individualist to work happily with committees. Imagine our dilemma when Aubrey Stephens offered to lend us £2,000 interest free if we would carry out the plans for the extension. In our usual foolhardy manner we went ahead.

Paul Armfelt recalled in the *Globe* anniversary booklet:

> I'm afraid I no longer have the drawings I made for the new auditorium which replaced the original much smaller seating area that we had. It was a relief to get those concrete block walls up, even though they were definitely not waterproof, and to see the new raked floor on those magnificent 16 x 2 kauri beams which Patric had scrounged from who knows where.

In the Christmas holidays of 1964, the troops were summoned all over again. More excavations were dug, concrete blocks carted, woodyards explored, and endless telephoning announced working bees. For me there were more pots of tea to make along with biscuits or what I called my stodge cake, evolved principally from crunched up stale cake or buns with a bit of dried fruit and spices. If served at once it was delicious, and there was never any left over.

The new extension provided for a workshop below ground level, a raked auditorium with space for costumes that had hitherto cluttered every corner of the house, and a reasonably sized foyer with a tiny area under the stairs for the box office and coffee. Upstairs there was a lighting box overlooking the stage, and a small dressing room. (Formerly, casts had all dressed in the 'little studio' in the house and this has continued when large numbers are involved.)

You will note that I say 'dressing room' in the singular. At first there was what we called a 'modesty curtain' slung across one corner but it didn't last long. How actors managed to compose themselves in these conditions for the long and difficult roles they played, I could never understand. In order to have a little time with the children, I generally dressed in my bedroom, even though I regretted missing the witty conversation and wonderful camaraderie that existed in the dressing room.

The enlarged Globe was not only functional, it was visually exciting as well. In the basement of one of the local decorating firms Patric discovered rolls of flock wallpaper at a ridiculously cheap price. As a result we had a beautiful green and gold floral design on the back wall, and apricot stripes along part of the side with the rest covered in Italian tapestry cloth. The foyer was coral pink with a classic Sanderson design. The concrete block wall down one side of the auditorium remained uncovered, maintaining the sharp acoustic quality which was such that the New Zealand Broadcasting Service (as Radio New Zealand was known then) recorded jazz concerts in it, led by Calder Prescott and the late Dick Hopp, rather than in their own studios.

We bought pink lampshades for wrought iron wall brackets in the foyer and auditorium, though what became of them I do not know. Sadie Foote, one of our most ardent supporters, provided new carpet for the foyer and staircase. We had enough donated rose-coloured velvet curtains for the foyer windows. At one end Patric built a charming little alcove to house our statue of Clio, who had hitherto resided in our front hall. One night at about eleven o'clock, after a particularly arduous day, Patric asked me to help him load Clio onto a wheelbarrow in order take her to her new home in the theatre. When I asked if she could wait till the morning, Patric's reply was that if I didn't want to help he would move her by himself, and I knew he would do just that. The next time Clio was moved, it took eight men to do it.

One of our members located a set of tip-up seats discarded from a church hall. This was very pleasing to the fire chief as they could be screwed to the floor. We had duly complied with the fire regulations that demanded an exit with a crash-door through the concrete block wall, but had carefully avoided installing a fire door between the theatre and the house until very much later when funds allowed. The stupid thing was that no sooner had we screwed down our handsome tip-up seats than it was claimed that egress was unsatisfactory. Whereas it would have been perfectly easy to arrange free access at the end of each row, the fire chief insisted we divide our precious front rows, which were longer than the others, but which were only about half the length of those in many other theatres. The result was that we lost half a dozen or so of the best seats in the house!

We still had to make do with oil heaters, as Christopher remembers. When he was a very small nervous seven-year-old, it was his job to light them – to go into the dark eerie theatre, up the stairs, and through the dressing room to the control room to put on the master switch before turning on the lights.

Later we installed central heating, which was a great help, especially in the cold Dunedin winters. Unfortunately it was very noisy and drew many complaints from our patrons. A new system is one of the many improvements that have happened since our departure from Dunedin.

Donald McAra, school teacher, artist, and later lecturer at Christchurch College of Education, who had a long association with the Globe as a member of the audience before leaving Dunedin, spent most of the Christmas holidays of 1964 working with Patric. In the anniversary booklet he reminisced:

> The house in London Street – pre-Globe. *The Chairs* of Ionesco. The tiny room could hardly contain the wild sense of pataphysical release – fresh air seemed to blow out the window at staid and stolid bourgeois Dunedin!

> Someone saying to Patric, 'Has anyone ever told you, you look like Jesus Christ?' Patric: 'My dear, I am Jesus Christ!'

> Rosalie as a crisply elocuted [I shudder at the word] Clytaemnestra – quite frightening actually. A lady of hidden drives, and very real warmth under the colourful theatrical manner she cultivated on the surface. The hospitality, the generosity, the willingness and supportiveness of the Globe, the Careys in particular, in encouraging the rank amateur. Fair enough sometimes there were pretensions, but so often they were well-used … Rushing up and down from the Octagon to pick up yet another sharpened circular-saw blade for cutting up stout, secondhand timber to build the staircase up to the back of the auditorium. The whole idea suddenly jelling, and my going back to Christchurch to build a facsimile Globe Theatre into the back of my largish classroom at Linwood High School.

I was fortunate in being able to see this fine construction, and remember Donald's enthusiasm as he recounted the effect on his students when Shakespeare was performed, or even just read, on the two-tiered stage.

Donald built the greater part of the staircase for the enlarged Globe and, when it was finished, who should offer to lay the carpet but Nicholas Zisserman! Like many White Russians, Nicholas had had a sheltered youth and was totally unpractical. He had never used a hammer before, but far from taking advice from those who knew something of what they were doing, he started the operation from the top stair leaning downhill to hammer in the tacks. The result was that not once, but several times, he overbalanced and landed in a heap at the bottom.

We were proud of our new extension and looked forward to audience reaction. The official opening was to be the first night of two short plays by Harold Pinter – *The Collection* directed by Pamela Pow, and *The Lover* directed by Michael Noonan. Michael Neill (Sam's brother) was in the cast. As it was a guest production, we particularly wanted to have everything in order.

About half an hour before the opening there was a cloud-burst and once again the roof let us – and the water – down. It was not just that rain was coming down in buckets – it was coming into the baby's bath, the preserving pan, and every possible receptacle in the place! Optimistically, I put towels in them to deaden the sound and Patric hastily slung a curtain in front of the waterfall, thereby cutting off the new part of the building from the tiny audience. In the interval I rushed to and fro emptying the water. The trouble was that the ridge where the new roof met the old had not been properly sealed.

There were times when we thought professional labour would be a blessing but that could have its problems too. To quote from my own contribution to the anniversary booklet:

> When the extension was added to the theatre there was the usual delay before the plumber came to put on the guttering – a job we felt beyond the scope of our amateur builders – and until he came the malthoid couldn't be fastened down. One horribly dark wintry night while Patric was away there was a healthy storm. After rehearsal David Mitchell and I went up the ladder carrying bricks. The wind was howling and I was terrified. We found malthoid sheets floating four feet above the surface of the roof. What an exercise, to capture it without it tearing. We carried enough bricks up the ladder to hold it down in face of the wind and RAIN!

Around this time the National Film Unit made a documentary about the theatre, and as we moved from area to area I shot ahead to lay papers and mats in the pools of water underfoot. When the plumber finally did arrive, he turned back the malthoid round the edge of the building but failed to put it back. My prize exhibits that winter were the snow white toadstools growing under the table in the foyer.

More assistance – amateur or professional – would have been

welcome on many occasions such as when Patric hauled eight by eight (inch) ceiling beams into position on his own, by means of a rope. No wonder he developed an ulcer.

Patric was not the only zealot, though. Betty Ussher, for example, upholstered all seventy-three of the tip-up seats. Initially Betty refused to come to the theatre because of the idolatry exercised by some of her friends. 'I wasn't going to walk over broken bottles for Patric Carey,' I heard her say. And what were her later thoughts about the theatre?

> I learnt more from the Globe Theatre than I had ever learnt at school. The people were – on the whole – so inspiring and so kindly. Meeting Mícheál MacLiammóir for instance!

(During Mícheál's visit to Dunedin with his solo portrayal of Oscar Wilde, Patric was invited to interview him on radio; he spent quite a bit of time with us and became our patron.)

> It was a world apart. Beautiful lighting from Neill Walker – beautiful music – fascinating sets and always Rosalie working in the background and Patric to the fore. I have never found that world again … I remember entering a dark theatre and seeing Patric in the lights box, and at the very top of the auditorium Belinda quietly playing the recorder. It is impossible to pick out 'anecdotes'. It has for me to remain as a whole, with the Carey magic pervading everything and keeping a miraculous balance.

Betty appeared in a number of plays, her greatest challenge being the long role of Winnie in Samuel Beckett's *Happy Days*. Winnie spends her days 'up to her neck in sand', her thoughts dwelling on nothing but the mundane things in her immediate environment.

Later when Betty and her family went to live in Timaru she staged a number of the plays she had met at the Globe in her drawing room, and ultimately persuaded the local drama society to build an intimate theatre, in which I performed much later.

My happiest recollection of 1964 was Patric's production of *Hamlet*. It was a slightly trimmed version set in the nineteenth century, that being the latest date we felt sword fights would be credible. We were fortunate in having Peter Clare as fencing master to coach our actors and students. (We had had a set of foils and masks donated to us and on Saturday mornings held classes in the garden – weather permitting.) This time we had a group of trained actors with Beverley Pollock as Gertrude, and Dallas and John, who were now husband and wife, as Hamlet and Ophelia.

For her wedding, Dallas had an exquisite gown with a drape and train at the back that suggested the 1880s, and I based the costume design around it. At first Dallas liked the idea of wearing it for the play but being so newly married she felt she could not quite bring herself to subject her precious dress to the exigencies of being worn on the stage. Reluctantly I found an alternative, but when I mentioned this to her later, she said, 'How ridiculous! It finished up in the dress-up box for my daughters!'

By this time our audience was much more appreciative, not the least being Donald McAra, who had come from Christchurch to see it. *Hamlet* was his favourite play. He wanted to play Horatio. The cast so enjoyed the production that we decided to revive it the following year. By then our Horatio had gone overseas but we arranged dates to coincide with the May holidays and Donald was able to come down to play the part. The inevitable lack of rehearsal drew these comments from him:

> The chance to appear as Horatio to John Fairmaid's Hamlet ... throwing him wrong lines which he improvised his way out of with extra lines the Bard would have been proud of! I seem to remember a remarkable Polonius in that production [John Dawson] – and a Ghost that creaked round in black polythene ...

Dallas and John became a great team both on and off the stage. Both also had successful professional careers, but they said goodbye to the stage after we left the Globe. (They have recently retired to Central Otago to plant olives.)

During our years at the Globe, Dallas appeared in no less than twenty-nine productions with John in almost as many. Not long after *Hamlet* they featured in Tennessee Williams' *Suddenly Last Summer* with John as the psychiatrist and Dallas as Catherine, the young girl who had been traumatised by watching the ritual killing of a homosexual.

Suddenly Last Summer is a shortish play – just as well, as it is so emotionally charged. Williams wrote *Something Unspoken* to precede it. Fortuitously, Peggy Freeman, who had toured with the New Zealand Players, contacted us at this time. Her health was not good, but she felt she must be involved in theatre again and enquired if she could work backstage. Patric cast her in *Something Unspoken* opposite Edith Mercier. Edith's ex-husband was in Patric's first production for the Repertory Society, and she and her family have been pupils, actors, backstage and front-of-house helpers and friends ever since.

Peggy was a fine actress with a warm personality and musical speaking voice, and Patric enjoyed working with her. Towards the end of the year he cast her in the beautiful role of Arkadina in Chekhov's *The Seagull*. We wanted Bill Mackay, a talented young man who had been a pupil of mine for some years, to play Arkadina's son Trepilov, but the production was very near to university examination time.

Patric discussed the matter at length with lecturers and with Bill, who ultimately decided in favour of playing the part. Academic studies were not for him. He wanted to be a professional actor. This never came about. He made a career in the visual arts instead. His paintings may be seen in the Victoria University library and his murals on a variety of public places in Wellington.

We revived *The Seagull* for Festival Week the following January, but Peggy's asthma made us wonder if she would complete the season. Being the trooper that she was, she struggled through.

It was not only Peggy we watched with trepidation. One of our more daring members had not been satisfied with the stuffed seagull we used in the first season, and took it upon himself to break the law and shoot a real one. We had no suitable refrigerator ourselves, so after each performance the feathered corpse was taken home by a member of the cast and brought back for the next performance. By the last night it was far from fresh and the smell quite appalling. I pitied the people in the front row, which is almost on the stage.

After the show we buried what was left of the poor bird under the 'Uncle Walter' rose bush, which responded with a galaxy of flowers – a fitting memorial to dear Peggy who died only a few months later.

By mid-1964 I had instituted regular weekly gatherings where 'anyone with hands' was welcome to have morning coffee – or tea – and help with sewing, addressing envelopes, folding newsletters, gardening or theatre-cleaning. Peggy came as long as her health permitted and took a childish delight in being challenged to make a smoking jacket for Paul Armfelt to wear in *Uncle Vanya*. Discovering hidden talents was certainly an important aspect of the Globe.

The long-term members of my Tuesday morning group included an elderly gentleman, Joe Beach, who had a puckish sense of humour and kept the ladies entertained; Doreen Graham, who came in from Mosgiel; and Sadie Foote, a retired librarian. All three have since passed away.

Sadie was a singularly loyal supporter – I doubt if she missed one production. Very well read, she had a passion for Shakespeare going back to her days with the Dunedin Shakespeare Reading Society (inaugurated in 1877, the first of its kind in the Southern Hemisphere). The *modus operandi* was for actors to stand on the stage of Burns Hall – the men in tails or dinner suit, the ladies in long evening dresses, jewellery and furs – to read the immortal words. Two or three of their number were happy to perform with us, but Dunedin's general attitude was that Shakespeare was not meant to be acted on a stage!

On one occasion as I ushered the daughter of the founder of the society to her seat at our production of *The Taming of the Shrew*, she looked around the half empty Burns Hall and remarked, 'Why don't you do a good comedy?' I replied that I had always thought *The Shrew* was an excellent comedy, but pointed out that the best box office returns we had ever had were for Sophocles' *Antigone* and *Oedipus Rex*!

Patric regularly took delight in arguing with Sadie on the merits of the bard, claiming that Webster was much better. Shakespeare, according to his argument, was not a good dramatist, even though Patric was in his element directing Shakespeare's plays, researching architectural designs, comparing texts, solving problems, and finding fascinating little anecdotes for the delectation of his casts.

He and Sadie also argued the merits and demerits of television. Patric rarely saw a programme on the box, but a friend had made a kitset model for Sadie. Living alone, she found it great company. Sadie had the last laugh. In her will she left a little money to our children, a painting to me, and to Patric she left the television.

In spite of the new challenges, 1964 had been a remarkable year of great plays and wonderful people, a highlight being Patric's beautifully restrained production of *Uncle Vanya*. Paul Armfelt was suitably cast in the title role – the loveable decadent personification of pre-revolution Russian aristocracy. Heather Douglas, a keen member of the Phoenix Players, gave a sensitive performance of the famous role of Sonia, Vanya's niece, frustrated in love and by her uncle's lack of will, finding consolation only in her loyalty to him and work on the estate.

Along with the lion's share of the building programme, Patric still did most of the directing. To quote Beryl Jowett (of whom more later):

> As well as the plays Patric had created a host of fabulous sets. There was never a disappointing one, and who could forget the rain forest at stage right for Tennessee Williams' *The Night of the Iguana* that seemed to emanate damp heat; or the stone cottage for Sean O'Casey's *Playboy of the Western World* – scrumpled paper and spray paint; and some of the elegant drawing rooms he established for Ibsen and Chekov, often denuding the Carey house of furniture or curtains.

Patric's wide knowlege and love of music was also important to the presentation of the plays. And he invariably made his own sound tapes too, operating the system himself. Radio New Zealand staff were often able to pirate sound effects for us, but only from what they had in their files. That hardly extended to the sound of two people jumping into a lake, needed for Ionesco's *The Chairs*. We tried all manner of ideas, the nearest being dropping a brick into water in the washing machine.

Another time, we spent a whole morning trying to create the sound of sleigh bells in the snow for a Chekhov play. We shook every conceivable object in a variety of containers until at last I unearthed a jester costume hung with little brass bells that my mother had made when I was a child. By shaking this up and down on a cushion on the floor we achieved an effective result.

We were fortunate in that from pre-Globe days most of the lighting was in the hands of Neill Walker, an artist in his own right. Tony Fergusson, an expert in electronics, did almost all the wiring as well as taking his turn in the lighting box. His mother, Susan, was a professional dress designer and took on many of the more complicated wardrobe and upholstery tasks. Much later – in 1972 – Lloyd Smith joined the team as did Charmian Dodd, whom he later married.

Charmian first appeared at the Globe when she was about twelve years old. In the anniversary booklet she recalled:

> When I left St Hilda's in 1965, several of the girls were having private lessons, so I did too. I remember being in a children's show. Just when she was supposed to go on stage, a little girl was found vomiting in the garden. I was in an older group and so knew nothing about the play. [The children had made it up themselves but I had scripted it for them]. But Rosalie thrust a copy into my hand and I went on in her stead. I did lighting, stage managing, sets, props, wardrobe, sound, and took part in *The Father, The Temptations of Oedipus* and *The Devils*.

She was also in the Otago University Drama Society tour of Robert Browning sketches and poems, one of seven programmes I directed for the students. Charmian later made a real name for herself designing, making and caring for costumes for television as well as for the Globe, and as a feature writer for the *Otago Daily Times*.

As well as being concerned that Patric was doing more than was wise, I was feeling over-extended myself. I claimed that I was a 'Jill of all trades and mistress of none.' Our consolation was that we were a team and were able to be at home with our children.

Patric was happy producing the plays of his choice, but I secretly longed to be back on the stage – impossible under existing circumstances if I were to maintain the standards that I, and others, expected of me. Because of the splendid students I had, I took considerable satisfaction from teaching but felt that I needed a refresher course.

Disregarding the cost, I enrolled as an observer for visiting American Paul Baker's seminar for actors and directors in Wellington. Apart from the time Patric and I had conducted a ten-day drama course with Ronnie Barker under the auspices of the Adult Education Service in Auckland in 1959, I had not been back to the North Island and eagerly looked forward to the trip.

Patric was rehearsing Bernard Shaw's *In Good King Charles's Golden Days*, an amusing insight into the life of the Merry Monarch and his contemporaries. Eric Herd, Head of the Modern Languages Department, was an ideal Charles II, and we had John Hunter who heard about us when he was in Ghana! As Kneller we had Trevor Peters, reputed to be the most brilliant student in the Otago philosophy department, who later joined the television staff and was last heard of making blue movies in Germany. On one of his visits back to New Zealand Trevor told me he had come for two reasons – to see his ageing mother and to have a Socratic argument with Patric, 'Even though,' he admitted, 'Patric cheats.'

Marian and the late Les Coxhead, both tireless workers for the Globe, were also in the cast of *In Good King Charles's Golden Days*. (Les later became an energetic chairman of the Friends of the Globe Theatre. Marian, in her quiet way always a most valuable supporter, compiled our twenty-fifth anniversary booklet, published in 1986.)

Loath though I was to miss even a rehearsal of a Shaw play let alone one in costume, I was quite excited at the prospect of having a little break – but there was a rather different one in store for me. I found myself playing Louise, the French whore in *In Good King Charles's Golden Days*. It was a delicious role and worth the sacrifice.

I have always loved wearing period costume and often felt a degree of envy watching others disport themselves in clothes I had designed and maybe helped to make. As well I had generally coached them in appropriate deportment. For Louise I was able to adapt a beautiful gold dress Irene Adcock and I had made for Dallas in *Arms and the Man* and I looked forward to wearing it with aplomb.

Unfortunately, that winter was very cold and my bones were

suffering. My knees were misbehaving to the extent that at times the only comfortable way to negotiate our steep staircase (the house has a thirteen-foot stud) was on all fours.

Previously, when the fleshly envelope was bothering me, everything had come right as soon as I stood in the wings of the stage. But one night I pranced on believing all would be well, only to have my right knee give way under me. I played the normally very active scene glued to one spot, and gingerly hobbled off at the end of it. Far from receiving any sympathy from Patric, I was scolded for spoiling his production.

CHAPTER VII

The Young Fry

Children of the Globe Theatre

૨●

Refresher course or no, teaching became an increasingly important part of my life. Not only did it give us a small but reasonably steady income but, allied with Patric's inspired direction, having a pool of trained actors to draw on greatly enhanced the standard of our work.

Teenagers and 'The Children of the Globe Theatre', as they came to be called, were a valuable asset. As well as acting they helped backstage and front-of-house and in return were given an awareness of great literature, music, and the visual arts, since from the outset Patric arranged exhibitions of work from all round the country as well as from local up-and-coming artists.

Besides the usual exercises for relaxation, concentration, and imagination, and backstage activities, classes embraced theatre and costume history; music, dance and fencing; to say nothing of what was learnt about food, wine and conversation along the way. For many years Patric joined me for these classes and we all found his vast knowledge and original ideas a great stimulus. Later, though, he gave me little support.

Parents often became involved, not only as audience but behind the scenes, while some joined classes and appeared on stage as well. While our own children were very small my routine was three days a week at St Hilda's from 10 a.m. to 3.35 p.m. with a half-hour lunch break if I was lucky. From 4 to 5 p.m., sometimes later, I taught at home. One year, two days a week, boarders from St Hilda's were allowed to come to me from 7 to 8 p.m. And regularly, on a weekday evening or on Saturday mornings, there was the senior drama group which ranged from teenagers to grandparents.

There was plenty of talent among the students. Four of my senior girls, Gabrielle Johnston, Marilyn Parker, Maureen Edwards, and Carol Moxey (who already had speech diplomas) each taught a group of children. I tried not to take anyone under nine because I wanted a little time for my own children. Christopher already attended classes along with a little group of other boys who stayed with us for many years. Then when Belinda was a pre-schooler, one mother pointed out that if I took her daughter, Belinda would be able to join the class. I conceded to this but the little group was soon handed over to a pupil teacher till examination time, when they came back to me.

At the end of the year we five teachers presented a series of little scenes which I tied together with a story. We called the show *The Petulant Puppeteer*. It was seen by a member of the Council of the Association of Teachers of Speech and Drama (now Speech Communication Association), who arranged for the text to be published.

As I have already mentioned, several of my pupils appeared in Mary Middleditch's production of *Lady Precious Stream,* as they did in Moira Fleming's version of *The Pied Piper,* which she wrote for her primary school class. Our production was seen by a television director and a performance was arranged for a children's programme, using some of Moira's pupils and some of mine.

The television staff created a fabulous set with a live goat and a handsome game rooster wandering round it. After filming the director donated the rooster to me. Our children loved it. But every afternoon exactly at four o'clock when I began teaching at home, it would set up a raucous serenade right outside my window. I had had visions of it being our Christmas dinner but under these circumstances it became advisable to send it temporarily – as I thought – to the farm of a friend. Not surprisingly we never saw 'Cocky' again.

By 1965 I was able to cast about a dozen of my young ones alongside some of our most experienced actors in Dylan Thomas's *Under Milk Wood.* Always in search of new concepts, Patric had removed the original features of the acting area, replacing the projecting tarras and the casement windows with a straight balcony in the manner of Jouvet's theatre outside Paris. The window structures were still in the basement so I set one in the centre of the balcony for Captain Cat to sit in, and instead of the usual solo narrator used four of my bright young school girls as 'gossips' reporting what was happening in the town.

But it was in Lorca's *The House of Bernada Alba* that the girls of the senior group really showed their mettle. Marilyn Parker and Maureen Edwards were splendid, but it was Gabrielle Johnston as Adele in the dramatic scene at the end of Act II who made an impression I shall never forget. She was equally successful in Pamela Pow's sophisticated production of Feydeau's famous farce *Hotel Paradiso,* which followed shortly afterwards.

Towards the end of 1965, the Dunedin Technical College advertised for a director for a full-time drama course, at a very good salary. I duly applied. To establish a training school for actors in New Zealand had been my life-long ambition and this would be the fulfilment of a dream. I had a very promising interview with the principal and it appeared that the position was to be mine. Unfortunately the college had not yet become a polytechnic, and under existing circumstances my academic qualifications were inadequate. As there was no one available with a suitable background, the plan was abandoned. Most of the sixteen applicants immediately enrolled at the Globe Theatre School.

I had done a great deal of preparation for the technical college programme and it now seemed propitious to establish a full-time course in drama at the Globe. We assembled an excellent team of part-time tutors. Patric would take care of production, decor, theatre history and literature; Rodney Kennedy, who was also skilled in these fields was officially in charge of costume design and history; Ian Ralston and I would specialise in acting and voice management. As well we had John Casserley for dance, Professor Peter Platt for music, Tom Esplin for art, and Peter Clare as fencing master. Several of us were conversant with stage management, lighting and promotion skills so between us we could provide a broad spectrum of tuition.

We offered scholarships to full-time students, and diminishing fees to long-term ones, with certificates for those who had fulfilled a quite demanding programme of practical work on stage and behind the scenes. We also encouraged the acquisition of diplomas in speech and drama from Trinity College London and the New Zealand Speech Board plus practical experience in teaching as well as on the stage. John Casserley encouraged our students to join his classes – free – at the School of Physical Education, and the university English department was prepared to have them sit in on appropriate lectures. The cottage next door, which had been bought by the Friends, could be used for their accommodation and they would, of course, take part in the programme at the Globe.

Needless to say, we had applied to the Queen Elizabeth II Arts Council for funding. They were in the throes of restructuring and correspondence seemed to float away into the ether.

Such was the enthusiasm and devotion of our students that in order to support our application, Marilyn, Gabrielle, and Maureen travelled to Wellington at their own expense to apply for Arts Council drama bursaries, not for the enormous cost of travelling overseas but simply for the modest fees required to pursue their work at the Globe, concurrently with their academic studies. Their efforts drew a blank. But that was, I suppose, only to be expected and nothing to the disappointments we were to suffer later on. Of course, I realise now that the whole plan should have been much more firmly based but I felt a degree of urgency on behalf of the new influx of students as well as my long-term ones.

While all this was happening I was asked unofficially if I could teach at Knox Theological Hall. For me it was out of the question, but Patric had complained that he was tired of being confined to the house and theatre so I surreptitiously recommended him for the post. Professor Lloyd Geering, who was principal of the college, came to see Patric performing in the *Marat/Sade* (Kurt Weill and Peter Weiss) and after a stimulating conversation over coffee decided Patric would be a suitable voice teacher.

He realised the advantage of his budding clergymen being associated with, and perhaps involved in, the theatre. He was probably aware, too, that in pre-Globe days Patric had done a most successful guest production with the students, assisted by one or two of our more experienced actors. That was Archibald MacLeish's *J.B.* which was presented in Knox Church on rostra placed on top of the pews suggesting the boxing ring MacLeish required. Of this production the *Otago Daily Times* had said: '... one of the most remarkable dramatic presentations to be staged in Dunedin for many years ... The cast must be accorded the highest praise ....'

Patric was duly installed in a basement studio at Knox College and, being a free-thinker, was labelled by the staff 'The Devil's Advocate'. He enjoyed the half-hour walk to and from the college and the mental stimulus of the literature available as well as contact with the students and staff.

On the strength of this I left St Hilda's in order to concentrate on the Studio. Along with my theatre duties, this was more than enough. Six years later I was invited back to teach part-time at the college, by which time I too was glad of a little change of scene.

Studio members also featured large in Aristophanes' *Ladies' Day*, in which Dionysus insinuates himself into a ladies' retreat. In our production the god was played by Wayne Tourelle, whom we had already seen in Pamela Pow's immaculate production of *Hotel Paradiso*.

Wayne was 'discovered' when Pamela adjudicated a drama festival in Balclutha, where she saw this young man give an outstanding performance in *The Long Wait*, a play he had written himself. Wayne and his first wife Eileen had met while studying drama at John Kim's Canterbury Repertory Theatre Drama School in Christchurch but were living and working on Wayne's family farm in Kaitangata – a good two-hours' drive from Dunedin – a journey they had to make for all rehearsals.

The last night of *Ladies' Day* was Christopher's one hundredth performance and thirteenth birthday. It was a tradition at the Globe that one hundred performances should be celebrated with champagne and Christopher felt he should be no exception. At the end of the season he went home with the Tourelles for a holiday, nursing an uncomfortable head.

A short time after that, Dunedin television advertised for a trainee director. I advised Wayne to apply for the position. He was accepted and has had a successful career with Television New Zealand and South Pacific Films, both in New Zealand and overseas.

It was in *Ladies' Day* that we made our only venture into nudity. It is true that the young lady, Jan McConnell, was on the balcony, visible only from the waist up, and had little rosettes pasted on her nipples – but whereas it would mean nothing today, in 1967 in Dunedin it was singularly daring.

That year, in order to give direction to my adult course, I decided to explore the great ages of theatre history. Each of the twenty-five young people chose a topic from a selection that included drama, art, music, costume, food, weaponry, and witchcraft. Information was submitted by the students through demonstration, illustration, or reportage.

In September the Association of Teachers of Speech and Drama had their conference in Dunedin for the first time, and for this we put the best of the assembled material into a two-hour programme entitled *A History of Costume and Manners*. After all this time I am still hearing warm recollections of the occasion. Later we condensed the material to half-an-hour for Dunedin television's afternoon session. This was followed by other costume-related programmes.

Joy Payne, council member of the Association of Teachers of Speech and Drama and examiner for the New Zealand Speech Board, was so impressed by our presentation and activities at the Globe that she arranged for her daughter Robyn to stay with us for four weeks, to be in a play and learn as much as possible. Had we been able to offer her a recognised qualification it would have been for at least a year, but under the circumstances she very wisely went to NIDA in Sydney. After some time teaching at the Western College of the Arts in Perth, she recently spent several years as Director of the New Zealand Drama School in Wellington.

Another actor who saw merit in working at the Globe was Ragini Werner. As a result of political pressure in Indonesia her parents, Ludwig and Thea, had brought their family to Dunedin where they set up a studio of dance. (Their son Frederick was for some years understudy to Nureyev.) Ragini acted professionally in Amsterdam, and on her return to New Zealand, worked with a small company in Auckland where her parents were then living. A motor accident had left her with one stiff knee and she lacked the confidence to apply for work in the professional theatre. She asked if she could stay with us for a month to see how she would cope on the stage. There was nothing for her in the Globe schedule but she came to classes and took part in a programme I was preparing for the second Dunedin Conference of the Association of Teachers of Speech and Drama, in which I tried to show how a selection of scenes might be played set in different eras.

I was very ill at the time and everything went wrong, including a last-minute change of venue from the Globe to Allen Hall. The speech teachers felt our theatre would be too small for their audience. We started late due to a prolonged annual general meeting; Christopher, who was playing an important part, was angry because he had arranged to ride to Christchurch on his motorbike after the show; Ragini was distressed because, although she had mastered walking smoothly in a crinoline on a flat stage, Allen Hall had a step onto the apron of about ten centimetres. As she moved downstage I held my breath. To my amazement, to say nothing of Ragini's, the stiff knee bent and she began to walk normally from then on.

If Auckland believes that nothing of significance happens beyond the Bombay Hills, Wellington believes there is nothing beyond Wellington; but irrespective of what Wellington felt about us, our reputation spread well beyond the confines of Dunedin.

When I adjudicated a drama festival in Christchurch I was impressed by the performance of a young girl – Helen O'Grady – playing the lead in Elmwood Players' outstanding production of Oscar Wilde's

Salome. I must have made some impression on her as well, for shortly afterwards she wrote enquiring about the possibility of coming to Dunedin to sit her LTCL in speech under our guidance and working at the Globe. Her parents wisely insisted she complete her course at teachers college and her PA year, which she did, then she decided to come. We were fortunately able to offer her good roles in Patric's production of *Twelfth Night* and in my *Too True to be Good* by Bernard Shaw. She took part in other plays at the Globe and also gained experience elsewhere. As well she assisted with teaching children and attended all group and adult classes.

When asked if I could recommend someone to front a television show Helen was the obvious choice. From there she went to Australia and after hosting a children's breakfast progamme, for which she wrote the music as well as the scripts, she went to Perth and opened a studio. Within a few years she had a staff of sixteen and was franchising drama courses in several countries.

About the same time I received a letter from Tonga, from Simon O'Connor who was approaching the end of his Voluntary Service Abroad, enquiring about our full-time course with a view to becoming a professional actor. There were no fancy brochures but I sent the relevant information explaining that no financial assistance was available, but suggested he should contact us when in Dunedin. Having returned to his home in Hamilton, he hitchhiked South.

'But when I got there,' Simon told me later, 'I was too scared to go and see you. I stayed at the Leviathan' [a private hotel] 'till I'd spent all my money.'

However, he did come eventually and stayed with us till he found a job; he took small parts but soon progressed to larger and more demanding ones. He passed a speech examination with honours, and impressed us with his skill as a writer. But he had to earn a living so could only be with us in evenings and on weekends.

Later he acted at the Playhouse, for the Fortune, Downstage, and Mercury. As well as several plays, he wrote scripts for television, and subsequently took over the playwright's course at Otago University from Roger Hall. Recently he gave an impressive performance as the father in the film *Heavenly Creatures*.

In June 1992 in an interview for the *Otago Daily Times*, Simon recorded:

> I turned up on their [the Careys'] doorstep and spent three years learning heaps from Rosalie and Patric, and not only from them, but also from the

huge variety of people that seemed to cluster round the Globe then ... It was a very interesting time for a guy of nineteen and it planted lots of seeds ...

Rather than say more about the studio myself, may I quote again from the *Globe* anniversary booklet, where Marilyn Parker, who has continued to work at the Globe ever since, wrote:

My memories of the Globe are memories of the place where I was educated. From the beginning of my last year at school when I raced gracelessly down the bank at the back of Littlebourne Ground to unlace Agamemnon's sandals, through my university years, and on and off ever since, I have seen the Globe as somewhere I was at home. But the most special years are the early ones when, every Friday night, Rosalie and Patric ran their senior drama class, and gave us the most wide-ranging liberal education available, I suspect, to teenagers anywhere in New Zealand at that time. We looked at paintings, listened to music, talked to artists of all types, and were expected to listen and question intelligently and quickly. Practice came through the numerous invitations to 'stay on and eat with us' when one had spent a day sewing costumes and painting sets. We were Mother Carey's chickens and both she and Patric looked after us well, unobtrusively shielding us from a lot that went on but making sure we had space to spread our wings and develop our confidence in many areas. Memories? Yes, of course. Doing the sound for *The Seagull* and confidently listening to Kostia's piano, unaware that it was playing only in the sound box. Huddling over the heating vents in the foyer in winter, production after production, waiting for the cue to go upstairs and pick my way across buckets under the leaks.

Words. The opportunity to be drunk on them week after week and some of the most enduring friendships of my life. A place to grow!

CHAPTER VIII

Enlarging the Pool

Working Together: Theatre – University – Television

૨ᴥ

As well as our excellent town-and-gown relationship with the university, we had the greatest co-operation from Dunedin radio and television. There was interchange with properties and costumes, and one year I provided almost all the costumes for nineteen programmes of *Music Hall* for television as well as having the fun of taking part in a couple of episodes.

The staff were not only regular members of our audience, but many trod the boards as well; for instance, in Synge's charming comedy *The Playboy of the Western World*, Hilda Bamber played Pegeen Mike while Rod Cornelius, who became Corporate Director of Resources for Auckland's TV1, was a most endearing Playboy, the young man who curried favour with all the girls because he boasted he had killed his da' – until the dad made an unexpected arrival on the scene. Our children thought Rod was wonderful, so much so that for his eleventh birthday Christopher wanted nothing more than to have him to dinner.

Whatever else happened during the daily round Patric somehow managed to keep up with a great deal of reading, and I well remember one particular day when he came back from town with a new play. Without even sitting down, we both read it right through gasping at the brilliance of the dialogue. It was Edward Albee's *Who's Afraid of Virginia Woolf?* We were about to embark on yet another New Zealand première.

Fortuitously, Colin and Eve Durning and their family had recently returned from the United States. Colin was dean-elect of the Dental School, but very sympathetic towards the arts. In spite of having borne seven children Eve was slim and beautiful. As well as her many other talents she had experience in acting, and while in the States had acquired a slight American accent. Patric cast her as Martha with American librarian Richard Hlavac as Nick. Honey was Rosemary Groube, daughter of Nancy Russell, a speech teacher who gave many years of wonderful drama to Hawera and surrounding districts in Taranaki. But who was to play Martha's husband George – 'the bog in the History department'? We launched into rehearsals hoping for the best.

One day while I was teaching there was a ring on the telephone. The caller was a gentleman enquiring about my drama classes – to my surprise not on behalf of some child, but for himself. It was a good voice, so I leapt in and asked politely what sort of age he was. He told me, adding that he might look a little older.

'Slightly balding?' I enquired hopefully. He replied in the affirmative.

'Can you do an American accent?' He thought so.

I said, 'How soon can you come and see me? I may have a part for you.'

Neil Gunn duly reported and was ideal. He had considerable difficulty learning lines, but with a great deal of support from other members of the cast, he succeeded.

Patric built a fabulous set with a curved staircase made of angle-iron, sweeping down from a narrow balcony. Eve made exciting clothes for herself, and in one scene wore a most glamorous off-one-shoulder evening dress of mine – of no use to me in Dunedin's chilly climate. In another she wore a trouser suit with a top of apricot silk and lame tapered trousers – all very new to us in those days.

In order to hold our own with Downstage Theatre in Wellington, the Friends and I arranged a buffet dinner before opening night. Patric disapproved. His attitude was firmly that 'the play's the thing' and it was unfair to the cast to have a party first.

Of the show itself author O.E. Middleton wrote in our anniversary booklet:

> I recall with particular pleasure the splendid acting of the cast of four in a scintillating production of *Who's Afraid of Virginia Woolf?*

His opinion was undoubtedly shared, for attendance was particularly good. Like most of Patric's productions the acting was restrained – very different from the film version which came later. When we revived it for an Arts Council delegation, they did not like our interpretation one little bit.

In 1965, having freed myself from St Hilda's, I was able to take a more active part at the Globe. I thoroughly enjoyed the production of *Under Milk Wood*, which I have already mentioned. Later in the year I was cast as one of the three 'initiates' in Patric's second production of

The Frogs (Dudley Fitts' translation).

Towards the end of the year I felt Patric must be given a break. Pamela Pow's double bill, August Strindberg's *The Creditors* and *The Stronger*, had been the only other guest productions, and Patric had already done seven. Since it was on our schedule and since I had read few other plays that year, I directed N.F. Simpson's *One Way Pendulum*, an English example of the Theatre of the Absurd.

The play demanded one-hundred-and-one weighing machines, one of which was vocal. The quiet ones were easily depicted by projections on the concrete auditorium wall, but being totally without mechanical knowledge I was at a loss to know how to manage the other one. Les Groube, a lecturer in anthropology, who was playing the mad scientist responsible for the machines in the play, advised me not to worry, and at the dress rehearsal he arrived with a fantastic creation which incorporated all the necessary requirements including a loud-speaker for recorded sound. Tony Fergusson decorated it with lights that flashed at appropriate moments – well, most of the time anyway.

I was particularly pleased that there was a good part for Marilyn Parker. At school she was always a tall poppy both physically and intellectually, but she had arms that bent back abnormally at the elbows that her young friends teased her about. In *One Way Pendulum* she had to say, 'How can I go out with arms like this?' and she was sport enough to demonstrate this peculiarity for the benefit of the play.

Trevor Peters played the Judge. At one awful moment he paused after pacing the floor while making his deliberations, looked down from his not inconsiderable height to the black-and-white tiled floor of the stage, and saw a tiny black kitten right in middle of a white tile. Goodness knows where it had come from. Double-jointed arms could not raise a laugh comparable with this!

Had it been a white cat his surprise would have been much less for our cat Wibble-Wobble was well-known to all our actors. She was named after the little boat in a William Clausen ballad, because when she was hit by a piece of wood during building operations it left her with a stiff pelvis that gave her an extraordinary sexy walk. She and her sister were a Christmas present to the children from Irene Adcock. It was the children's job to ensure that both cats and their offspring were secure in a bedroom before every performance. Wibble-wobble got crafty and would hide until a crucial moment in a play, when she would stroll across the stage to a heating vent under a seat in the front row.

Choosing a cast is perhaps the director's most important task. Given a good play and good actors, how can one fail? Experienced artists can adapt to a variety of characters but with the less experienced, particularly in intimate theatre, type-casting is not only inevitable but, generally speaking, desirable – though we tried to be subtle about it.

To quote Gay McInnes, author of the popular novel *Castle on the Run:*

> Renowned for his tongue-in-cheek type-casting Patric had me playing bitchy, middle class American women, as in Edward Albee, or po-faced Chekovian women, all forlorn and sighing for Moscow, to a boozy, blowsy harpie in Tennessee Williams. For Patric Carey was nothing if not an under-cover psychotherapist.

Nevertheless she goes on to say:

> 'Where else could we have learned so much about ourselves in such a charming setting and all for free!'

Most decisions about the theatre were arrived at by discussion between Patric and myself, but when in doubt I tried to let him have the final say. After all he was the driving force. Casting was one area in particular where he sought my co-operation, but when it came to *Saint Joan* he had a fixed idea which gave me some concern.

At the University Book Shop was a very shy, very pretty girl who worked very hard for the theatre but who had told me she had no ambition to go on the stage. Patric insisted she should play *Saint Joan.* Fortuitously I met Sandra Burt, another of the talented members of the television staff, in the street. She enquired if Saint Joan had been cast as she had played it at school and would dearly like to repeat the experience. (That is the thing about great plays; the more one works on them, the more one can learn and enjoy.) I had admired her performance in another theatre and could imagine her in the role. I had learnt not to argue with Patric in such situations so I suggested to Sandra that she should make Patric's acquaintance and recommended her to come to the first rehearsal of *Saint Joan* the following Sunday, ostensibly to help me with costumes. She duly reported but the other young lady did not. Sandra made a splendid *Saint Joan* and appeared in other plays at the Globe as well.

As I have said already, there was excellent co-operation between the Globe and the university, and it was posssibly Rodney Kennedy's student production of *The Queen and the Rebels* that led Patric to the plays of Ugo Betti, a rising Italian dramatist of the sixties who wrote in allegory with underlying political themes. In 1966 Patric wanted to do another of Betti's plays, *The Burnt Flower Bed,* but did not have a strong actor available for the leading role, and was himself already in the cast.

But then, via the grapevine, we learned that Ian Ralston, who had done such excellent work with us before, was 'resting' on his parents' farm at Outram, just out of Dunedin, after a long tour in *Oh What a Lovely War* with Theatre Workshop. This was an offshoot of The New Zealand Theatre Company, the successor to the New Zealand Players. Ian had been overseas for two years, studying at the Birmingham School of Drama and working in the professional theatre in England. He was now married to Judy Weller, a charming English girl, who was a keen amateur actress.

Patric took a bus to Outram. We had resolved that in view of Ian's professional status he must be offered a fee, but after the tour he had decided theatre was no longer for him. However, having recognised the quality of the play and out of respect for Patric, he accepted the part but refused any emolument. (That decision was a turning point not only for the Globe but for Ian's career, for he later joined television and has worked in the media on and off ever since.)

After *The Burnt Flower Bed,* which drew limited audiences but much credit, Ian flung himself into directing a revue and other plays, which along with a couple of other guest productions gave Patric some welcome respite.

One of these was a Phoenix Players' production of Christopher Fry's complex verse play, *The Dark is Light Enough,* directed by Mary Middleditch, with Beverley Pollock and Louise Joyce of television in the leading roles. Beverley had recently returned from England, where she had, among other things, been a tour guide at Anne Hathaway's cottage in Stratford-upon-Avon. Louise was a newcomer to Dunedin theatre, and she and Beverley made a great team.

The production had had a short season at the Playhouse but audiences were not good. We saw it and liked it very much, and believed it would have greater appeal for our clientele. We therefore invited the Phoenix Players not only to perform it at the Globe but to make our premises their permanent home. After all, several of their actors already worked with us, and we shared the same ideals.

Unfortunately Louise, who was working for broadcasting, was transferred before the second season. Other things went wrong and what Christopher Fry described as a 'dark' play became an even darker production. Sadly too it was Beverley Pollock's swan-song and virtually the end of this stoic little society. Mary Middleditch continued to produce plays periodically at the Globe and later became one of its artistic directors, but the 'Phoenix' had regrettably sunk back into the ashes.

Another unexpected challenge came my way in 1966. One Sunday, when my conscience was particularly troublesome over my neglect of the children, I made a great effort and took Belinda to Moana Pool, which was very close to our home. I had not the energy to swim myself, so I sat in the noisy viewing area trying to identify some little thing that could be taken out of my daily programme.

On our return home Patric said to me, 'You're playing Olia' – the eldest of Chekhov's *Three Sisters*. I explained that I was scheduled to adjudicate a five-day drama festival in Christchurch during the rehearsal period, but he said he could cope with that. The festival provided a change of scene and I had the usual exciting but exhausting time.

When I arrived back in Dunedin I would happily have gone to bed and stayed there for a week. However, I carried on regardless, as the saying goes. It would have taken a great deal to have kept me from appearing in such a beautiful play.

It was also in 1966 that John and Barbara Casserley joined us. They had just returned from the United States. Barbara was a trained ballet dancer; John specialised in modern dance and had come to Dunedin to set up a course at the School of Physical Education. This he did with great success, his early students including Gaylene Sciascia, Jan Bolwell and Jamie Bull, who are still making an important contribution to dance in New Zealand.

With the combined talents of the Casserleys and the Ralstons the Globe's achievements soared. In a galaxy of great plays and many unflawed productions, it is difficult to highlight particular ones, but there is no doubt that Peter Weiss's *The Assassination and Persecution of Marat as Performed by the Inmates of Charenton under the Direction of the Marquis de Sade* – otherwise known as the *Marat/Sade* – with its extraordinary characters, catchy songs and skilful dialogue made an impact far beyond Dunedin. Ian Ralston played Marat, John Casserley the lecher Duprès, while Patric was de Sade himself.

James Wright (who later became a professional actor in Australia) made a splendid Herald and we used the fine photograph of him taken by de Clifford James on our programme covers for many months. All told we had an excellent cast but the performance that stands out

Above: A rehearsal of Albee's Who's Afraid of Virginia Woolf?, *which was the New Zealand première in 1965. Left to right: Rosemary Groube, Patric Carey, Dick Hlavac, Neil Gunn.*
Below: Rosalie Carey, Maureen Edwards (left) and Eve Durning (right) as the Three Sisters, in the play by Chekhov, 1966.

Above: Lena Bratt (left) and Betty Ussher working on the lavish costumes for Lady Precious Stream, *by Hsuing, directed by Mary Middleditch, 1966.*
Below: James K. Baxter when first involved with the Globe, 1967.

in many of our memories was given by broadcaster and historian Judith Fyfe as the patient suffering from sleeping sickness in the role of Charlotte Corday. When we repeated the show the following year Judith came back specially from Masterton for the season.

A feature of the show is the idea of having the inmates of the asylum roaming about the auditorium (and in our case the garden as well) before the play and in intervals. Needless to say the young group was in full force as extras, responding well to instruction given by psychiatrist friends on the likely behaviour of the characters, and enjoying creating roles for themselves on and off the stage.

One night, an elderly professor came to the theatre with friends with whom he had been wined and dined. During the performance he had a slight heart attack. His friends escorted him to the foyer. Noticing something was amiss I joined them and supplied obvious help such as a drink of water. But I knew that Dr Morris, the Superintendent of Cherry Farm, the psychiatric hospital, was in the front row of the auditorium. I crept up behind him, tapped him on the shoulder, and asked if he could attend a patron who was ill. He ignored my first, second, and possibly third plea, but in the interval strolled into the foyer, and was shocked to see the elderly gentleman looking decidedly seedy. He apologised for his tardiness, but explained that his reaction to my request had been: 'These Careys! What will they think up next?'

The *Marat/Sade* played to full houses night after night as well as for the return season early the following year. One Saturday, Mervyn Thompson brought a party of ten from Christchurch. They dossed down in the theatre for the night and enjoyed a breakfast of bacon and eggs with us the following morning. Later Mervyn brought his version of the show to the Mayfair Theatre in South Dunedin. It was excellent in its own genre – greater emphasis on music and more like the film. Not long afterwards, Mervyn produced it at Downstage, and shortly after that became Downstage's director.

It was during the *Marat* season that James K. Baxter made his first visit to the Globe. He had been the Burns Fellow at the University of Otago for over a year, but was determined not to be tempted by the theatre till certain literary obligations were complete. I was in the kitchen, preparing supper, when James appeared at the back door exclaiming, 'Bloody marvellous! Good on yer!' and disappeared.

Thirty-six hours later he arrived with a script. He had been mulling over a play for several months but needed the time and inspiration to write it. It was called *The Band Rotunda*, and was the first of nine plays he was to write during the next two years, seven of which were premiered at the Globe. But more of these in a later chapter.

CHAPTER IX

A Turn of the Tide

The Arts Council looks the other way

之

Where there are highs there must be lows and we certainly had our share in 1966.

Bernard Esquilant and Bill Menlove had been given well-deserved bursaries to study theatre overseas. During their absence we were interviewed a couple of times on radio. Nothing was explained but the questions were slanted towards funding for the arts. Gradually we realised we were being sounded out about the establishment of regional theatres – an idea we had advocated for some time.

In Christchurch, Yvette Bromley had established a semi-professional group in a disused warehouse, but in October the Canterbury Theatre Trust was formed to set up a fully fledged professional company in the Repertory Theatre under the direction of John Kim. He was given funds to go overseas to recruit actors – though there was surely plenty of talent already in the country. He also received a $25,000 grant, plus $13,000 from the Queen Elizabeth II Arts Council, plus a loan of $10,000. Salaries ranged from $30 to $500 a week. It folded after only one year owing between $10,000 and $20,000. At the time the Globe had received $19,000 in all.

When Bernard and Bill came back, no doubt full of enthusiasm and inspiration, they also created a new structure and received official support. To quote David Carnegie writing in *Landfall* 136:

> The Southern Comedy Players, under the subtle coercion of the need for continued subsidy and with the aid of the short-lived New Zealand Theatre Centre, announced in 1966 its new name of Southern Players and its intention to employ full-time professional actors and directors, to present six to eight plays a year in its enlarged Playhouse and, significantly, to limit touring activities to Otago and Southland.

In other words the Southern Players were to be Dunedin's regional theatre. The reaction of the *Otago Daily Times* was:

The Globe, run by Rosalie and Patric Carey has, for a similar period as the Southern Comedy Players, given the kind of Theatre neither the Southern Players nor any amateur group has aspired to. Many considered it the proper base for regional development. In contrast to this a $1,300 Arts Council grant was given to the Globe. Last year however, the Globe got nothing at all.

It is easy to imagine our reaction and that of the Friends of the Globe.

Other blows were yet to come. One day I met Marilyn Parker in the street. She looked worried and said, somewhat shamefacedly, that she had been offered a part in *The Knack* (Anne Jellicoe) with the Southern Players. She was earning her university fees by working as a housemaid in a hotel, so of course it would have been ridiculous for her not to accept a professional engagement in the theatre. After all, what were those years of training for?

The final humiliation came when the Southern Trust was given the wherewithal to establish a full-time drama course at the Playhouse. They had engaged tutors such as John Casserley and Shona Dunlop, both excellent teachers of creative dance. But what really got my hackles up was that several of my most senior students were offered bursaries to attend the Playhouse drama course. I encouraged them to do so but they stayed only for a month or two and the school lasted not much longer.

Fortuitously, when I was in Wellington adjudicating speech competitions, I was able to see John Malcolm, Internal Affairs representative on the Arts Council. I pleaded that I felt they had mounted a campaign to close us down, and that as far as I personally was concerned, I would be happy for that to happen. Mr Malcolm's reaction was 'You are the beacon that lights the way for other theatres to follow.'

He assured me that something could be done. In no time at all a cheque for five hundred pounds arrived for the Globe 'in recognition of its unique contribution to drama in New Zealand in the ten years of its existence'. (This took into account our time as Rosalie and Patric Carey Productions before the theatre was built.)

The Southern Players had one successful year but problems ensued and Bernard and Bill were obliged to undertake a further extensive tour around New Zealand in order to balance the budget. The Southern Trust decided to buy the Playhouse. They brought actors from overseas, two of whom spent their leisure time at the Globe moaning about the situation at the Playhouse.

It transpired that we were not the only ones to be disgruntled. A group in Auckland calling themselves Artists for Action had formed to protest against the policies of the Arts Council, who, it appeared, expected the arts to be commercial enterprises. This gave Patric the lead he needed. He sent telegrams to Artists for Action and to the major newspapers, announcing that unless the Arts Council changed its outlook we would close the Globe.

The Auckland artists were delighted. They paid Patric's fare to Auckland, inviting him to speak to them. The night he returned there was a public meeting in our theatre where he reported on what had taken place. It was generally agreed that to close the Globe was unthinkable.

The university students in particular went into action. They gathered five hundred signatures (but no money of course), set up booths at the university to take bookings, and pursued an energetic membership drive. The trouble was the students occupied so many seats at fifty cents each, there was often no room for patrons who would have paid the full price!

The campaign was led by Peggy Jowett, whose family was very special to the Globe. I vividly remember their first visit in 1964. I was curating an exhibition in the theatre. Right at the end of a quiet afternoon a family arrived. I showed them around, and found them so interesting I invited them to have a cup of tea with Patric and me. Geoffrey Jowett was taking up a university lectureship; his wife, Beryl, is a potter; and by the end of the visit three of their four children were enrolled for drama classes.

In the *Globe* anniversary booklet Beryl had this to say:

The Globe Theatre was three years old when our family came to live in Dunedin, and was the first place we visited. Apart from the plays, my main memories are of the opportunities to view art and craft produced by the public, and by those whom the Careys felt had potential in their various fields, giving them the opportunity to exhibit their work in an interesting and stimulating environment. It was at the Globe that we first saw Colin McCahon's Waterfall paintings, Barry Brickell's truly indigenous pots, John Middleditch's drawing and sculpture, Lindon Cowell's all too rare paintings, to mention just a few; all shown with taste and the opportunity given to think and talk about the work displayed. People like myself who found it hard to promote their own work were invited to exhibit and I well remember the garden pot exhibition where the pots were displayed in the lovely old rambling garden, and looked so much at home there ...'

(To everyone's great satisfaction Beryl and Lindon Cowell made an exchange of several large pieces of art work, which they still enjoy today.)

Beryl continued:

I recall all the Dionysus badges Peggy and I made for a fund raising effort, and the many cups and saucers [seventy-five in all!] with the Dionysus design I made for after-the-show refreshments and how I had to make such flat saucers to fit into Rosalie's dish washing machine ...

And a very embarrassing experience at the Globe. We were in the audience one evening and I thought that sitting under a dripping roof was one thing, but the dreadful smell in the theatre that evening was quite another! When we got home we discovered that one of our sons had a very dead rabbit in his pocket he could not bear to leave at home!

Thank you Rosalie and Patric and all your helpers for the Globe Theatre.

The Friends of the Globe were already making a real effort on our behalf. Colin Durning was a dedicated chairman ably supported by Shirley Mackenzie as secretary. Shirley came to the Globe in 1965. She had listened to so much adulation from her friends, that she had thought: 'This makes me sick. Patric must be awful – over the top!'

But she finally came, met us and the theatre, and found that, as she told me when I visited Dunedin recently:

What had been said was all true! ... I had never been to the theatre before, so I took the Globe as the norm. After some years I went to another local theatre as a birthday present from my friends. To begin with, I was most impressed with the audience – the fur in particular! That was a revelation, but more was to come. The set – incredible by Patric's standards – was greeted with applause. Patric's sets supported, rather than overwhelmed, the play and created the appropriate atmosphere. When the leading actor appeared there was rapturous clapping. He played to the audience allowing extra time for droll moments marked by more adoring audience appreciation. This actor dispersed his largesse throughout the evening, each witty sally – especially the off-colour ones – being hailed by the captivated audience.

At the Globe there was no 'star' system – no matter how eminent the players, they were regarded only as essential to the play! The stunned silence that greeted a climax was louder than indiscriminate applause.

Shirley was a tower of strength. She, along with Colin and Eve Durning, the Coxheads and their friends set about a series of fundraising projects and took over other work for the theatre. For several years the Globe was on a roll.

I felt it would be an ideal time for us – the Careys – to take some sort of sabbatical leave, for I was confident that Ian and Judy Ralston could run the theatre more than competently, if we could find a way of surviving by other means. Even a year of a normal schedule in another theatre would seem like a holiday. Our playing seasons were still only ten performances and that meant averaging twelve plays a year over and above all our other activities. But we had no money, and what scope was there for people like us whose whole lives had been devoted to the theatre and associated skills? Perhaps, if we had had time to write letters and fill in forms, we would have sought help from the Arts Council, but we felt further pleas would be a waste of our waning energy.

Yet it so happened that we were about to embark on what, with hindsight, has been regarded as the most significant period of the little Globe's history.

CHAPTER X

Big Frogs in Our Pool

Baxter at the Globe

≥•

Following the threat to close the Globe, the Friends made a real effort to increase membership. To this end they watched the papers for new arrivals in the city, especially for university, broadcasting and television staff.

When Hal Smith came to take up a lectureship in the English Department, accompanied by his artist wife Els Noordhof and their four children, the Friends leapt into action. Els recalled:

> After arriving in Dunedin in 1967 from Boston, Massachusetts, we got involved in the Globe through Colin Durning (President of the Friends) who, one fine afternoon, knocked on the door of our motel unit and introduced himself as being on the committee of a small theatre at the top of London Street. He had read in the newspaper that we were interested in Drama and Painting and he wondered whether we would like to be part of it. So we looked in at London Street.
>
> There we met Patric and Rosalie Carey living in and around an enchanting small theatre standing in an imaginatively wild-looking garden. The conversations about theatre, literature and art around the big oval table in the back dining room with the walls covered by paintings (I remember the small waterfall by Colin McCahon) made us aware of what was going on artistically in New Zealand ... the walls of the theatre were full of paintings, all kinds. Young beginning painters mixed with more established ones, and Patric and Rosalie encouraged painters and potters to have exhibitions in the theatre. I had my first New Zealand exhibition mainly of drawings, in the Globe.
>
> After the exhibition I gave Rosalie and Patric the drawing of James K. Baxter whom I had met during the rehearsal of his plays.

And recalling his first encounter with the Globe, Hal chuckled when he told me of Colin Durning's invitation to meet Patric:

> 'When and how?' Hal asked.
> 'What about this afternoon?'

He picked me up and we went to see this man. Before we left, the bugger had cast me as Jock in *The Band Rotunda*.

Hal remembers the beautiful white rotunda with rounded canopy and balustrades with mixed feelings:

At the end of the play when I was supposed to be in the last stages of DTs from drinking methylated spirits – I was wearing a big heavy army greatcoat, and I had to clamber up the steps to the rotunda, spread out my arms like Jesus on the cross, and then collapse on the floor. After all that exertion I was quite puffed and I had to be there ostensibly without breathing while Concrete Grady made a very long speech. Boy, was I glad when the lights finally went out.

In the anniversary booklet he wrote:

The play is about a group of down-and-outs who have spent the night sleeping on or under a park bench. A light comes up representing sunrise. The cast look in its direction which in this case was towards the lighting box where Patric was operating the sound. I had to say, 'Y'know Jock I think I can see the sun. Looks like a pig's arse set around with parsley'. One night I looked up and there was Patric's face set around with a big black beard, pressed against the front glass of the lighting box, and all too aptly illustrated the line!

James K. Baxter came to every rehearsal and seemed delighted that Patric kept discovering phallic symbols whether or not he had thought of them himself.

Because of Baxter's colourful language and down-to-earth characters many of our older members were angered by *The Band Rotunda*, and indeed by all the Baxter plays that were to follow. Certainly anyone could sympathise with the elderly lady sitting in the front row of whom Hal Smith told me, 'One night when Jock Ballantyne – supposedly too crook to eat – took a healthy mouthful of fish he choked, projecting the unsavoury morsel into the lady's lap!'

One august matron vowed, 'If you do any more of those nasty Baxter plays I shall cancel my membership!' To which Patric replied, 'I shall do all the plays Baxter likes to give me.'

But Gwen Wales, who saw just about every play we did, told me, 'The last scene of *The Band Rotunda* was the greatest theatre I have seen. Sadie Foote and I felt so stimulated by those plays we would talk about them for days.'

That is exactly the reaction James and Patric had hoped for. Gwen continued:

The language didn't really offend me. It was abrasive and sharpened the wits. And we appreciated the symbols. I remember in *The Day That Flanagan Died* there were marigolds and carnations. I don't know if it was intentional, but those two are at the opposite end of the floral scale.

Whatever else, it is apparent we had developed a very perceptive audience. To quote Gwen's contribution to the anniversary booklet:

James K. Baxter and Patric Carey sat like two bearded gnomes knees hunched up under their chins in the garden and talked, talked, talked and talked. It could not be called conversation. It could not be called discussion. It went on endlessly in a crazy pavement pattern of days. Oh! for a tiny eavesdrop on the philosophy, wisdom, rancour and pithy gut roots of life they shared. Ever the gossip! But never the weather.

Sometimes these sessions would take place in our breakfast room and if I could arrange to be ironing or sewing I would eavesdrop as Gwen would like to have done, and it was as fascinating as she suspected. But more often they met at Stewart's coffee shop in the Octagon, drinking copious quantities of coffee or tea for Baxter was valiantly dealing with his alcohol problem and still had to cope with perpetual thirst.

Whatever the older patrons may have thought, the young people decided *The Band Rotunda* was just great. The characters may not have been typical of their day-to-day acquaintances, but they could identify with the feelings of loneliness and despair, and rejoiced in Baxter's use of the vernacular and recognisable locality. For myself, I found after watching Baxter plays that I experienced a new dimension the next time I saw a Chekhov production. Somehow I could appreciate more fully how Russian audiences must have felt when they saw – and heard – themselves on the stage for the first time after an artificial diet of mainly Parisian drama.

In *The Band Rotunda* the role of Snowy Lindsay (an elderly drunk) was played by Frank Grayson, whom Patric first met while directing Charles Morgan's *The River Line* in Timaru. Frank, then working as a shepherd, was a man of many skills and as stage manager for the local drama society made exquisite furniture and properties. John Dawson, for many years Chairman of the Friends, wrote of him:

The cream of Dunedin's Christmas shows in 1975 was Mary Middleditch's *The Snow Queen*. The hearts of the audience were melted by the realistic menagerie of loveable animal heads created by our artist-in-residence, Frank, the most inventive creator of fine stage-props I have ever met.

A cast sits mutually scratching its head: where can a black iron pot-bellied stove be found? Exit Frank, to return later with a creation of ivory-board, bits of wood and tubes from carpet-rolls that would fool anybody.

When the Southern Comedy Players were formed, Patric recommended Frank as stage manager. He stayed with the company for many years and afterwards worked for television.

Much later, after we had left the Globe, Frank lived in what had been our house, sharing it with wardrobe and properties and a beloved ancient cat. He became a valuable and much respected caretaker, set designer, writer, director and father figure, and at his death left his paintings and savings worth several thousand dollars to the Globe.

Soon after he had finished *The Band Rotunda*, James brought Patric a tiny newspaper cutting which he had nurtured for some time, as possible material for a play. It told of a family, living in a remote area, who belonged to a closed religious sect. When the sixteen-year-old son saw his mother embracing and dancing with the farm worker, rather than allow his sister to fall from grace in such a similar way, he killed her. Patric felt it had considerable potential and James came up with *The Devil and Mr Mulcahy*. I would like to have directed this play, as it was obvious that the young people should be played by two of my favourite students, Richard Mercier and Peggy Jowett. Patric insisted on directing, but I had my turn in Waipukurau many years later.

Having had two plays accepted for production and having found a compatible director, James was keen to continue writing for the theatre, but had no immediate ideas for a further plot. Patric reminded him that when T.S. Eliot was commissioned to write a play to commemorate the septuacentenary of Canterbury Cathedral he turned to the Greeks for his model, and suggested *Oedipus at Colonus*. After reading it James declared he was not yet ready – that, he vowed, would be his last play, and it was. But he did not abandon the idea of the Greeks as inspiration.

In the ensuing months he wrote six main-bill plays and several ten-minute ones, *The Hero* being the only short one to be printed in his collected works. Of the longer plays, Patric produced *The Sore-Footed Man, The Bureaucrat,* and *Mr O'Dwyer's Dancing Party* – all inspired by the Greeks. *The Day That Flanagan Died* developed from James' own ballad 'Lament for Barney Flanagan'.

Baxter's plays at this stage were all rather short for a whole evening. Patric preceded *The Band Rotunda* with Samuel Beckett's mime *Act Without Words* performed by Clive Bayliss. Inspired by this, John and

Barbara Casserley created new mimes to accompany other plays and Baxter wrote three himself.

At the end of this exciting series, the Casserleys and actor Stephen O'Rourke presented *An Evening with Baxter*, mimes and short dramas which they later took on tour along with a verse play, *Loose Boards and Seagulls*, by poet Peter Olds. It was a successful but arduous venture, and by the time they returned cracks had appeared in the Casserley marriage, heralding the end of this wonderfully creative team.

There were two other significant plays we didn't particularly care for, but Richard Campion did a spectacular production of *The Spots of the Leopard* at Downstage, and John Casserley directed *The Starlight in Your Eyes* for Otago University. Baxter also wrote three plays for radio before he left Dunedin.

Sometimes, in the Greek tradition, James used a chorus – such as three charladies in *The Bureaucrat*, and three sailors in *The Sore-Footed Man* – but for the most part he used the legend rather than the play itself, often introducing characters purely for dramatic effect. In *The Temptations of Oedipus*, for instance, he gave Antigone a baby – no doubt because he himself had just become a grandfather.

In *The Sore-Footed Man*, he introduced Eunoe, a wife for Philoctetes, as he explained to Frank McKay 'simply because I thought ten years a long time for a man to be on his own'. I had the privilege of initiating the Eunoe role with Ian Ralston as Odysseus and Patric as Philoctetes.

From the wardrobe I had elected to wear my favourite Greek costume – an off-one-shoulder sax-blue linen chiton hand-printed in silver. The season had already been postponed because Ian Ralston had the flu. We were now well into winter, and there was a major snowstorm. Not only were we very uncomfortable in our scanty costumes, but the storm kept the audience away in droves – a pity because it was probably our favourite of the Baxter plays.

When Patric and I read it we were both excited; when we rehearsed it, we liked it even more. Most of those who saw it felt the same, even though there was a shocked gasp when one of the three sailors sang, 'I'll have to eat shit'. It was reminiscent of the reaction to Eliza Doolittle's 'Not bloody likely', which is nowadays accepted without a qualm.

The Bureaucrat was based on the legend of Prometheus who was chained to a rock in the way that Baxter saw civil servants chained to their desks. For our production, a particularly large desk Patric had made for *Dial M for Murder* for the Repertory Society dominated the stage. (It normally served as a dressing table for me.) The office was built of angle iron in an asymmetrical shape, filled in with green plastic fruit trays destined for the tip. Lit from above they produced a strange sterile quality.

In *Mr O'Dwyer's Dancing Party* (produced late in 1968), the Dionysus figure is a creative drama tutor whom I suspect was based on John Casserley. His pupils are a group of Remuera housewives. Their scenes are action packed, whereas the beginning and end of the play are simply long philosophical dialogues between the husband of the hostess and a Jewish neighbour, who might well have been James and Patric in full verbal flight.

When James finally chose Sophocles' *Oedipus at Colonus* as his legend for *The Temptations of Oedipus,* he was already planning to leave Dunedin. 'I'm going to plant kumara at Jerusalem on the Whanganui river,' he told us.

For *Oedipus* we not only had a splendid line-up of principals – Ian Ralston, Ray Stone, Johanna Pereau, Cilla McQueen and Patric himself – but for the chorus of women Patric gathered together all our previous leading ladies. This galaxy of beautiful, talented women – Eve Durning, Dallas Fairmaid, Lyndal Howley, Frances Mulrennan, Nevan Rowe, Mari-Ann Irving, and Charmian Dodd – ironically spent most of the play hidden behind hand-held masks.

Ralph Hotere was the designer. For the costumes he did a series of attractive, if vague, watercolour sketches which Maureen Hitchings and Eve Durning translated into beautiful flowing robes. The paintings were exhibited during the season; the set, which Ralph built almost entirely himself, extended from floor to ceiling resembling a wonderful ice-cave, all made of white sheets of polystyrene. For backgrounds, he painted a series of abstract designs on coloured slides for projection onto the cyclorama. Anthony Watson (first Mozart Fellow at Otago University) wrote the music.

O.E. Middleton recalled:

> The result was impressive … *The Temptations of Oedipus* enabled me to see at close quarters the inner working of the Globe and the subtle blend of skills, personal integrity and rare talents that made it such a force for so long.

On the afternoon of the final performance I was acting as curator for the exhibition, when the fire chief appeared. We had made some attempt to comply with his requirements but we had neither the money nor the will to install a fire-door between the theatre and the house. I greeted him cordially, did a quick think and said, 'Just the person I want to see. We've taken out the seats, and put in the crash-door, but we couldn't remember what else you wanted us to do.'

But these things were not worrying him. He was concerned about the polystyrene set. Only the week before, two people had died in a fire in the Hutt Valley from fumes of burning polystyrene, and the conscientious fire chief decided we must remove the set or have him close the theatre down.

With the house fully booked, either alternative was unthinkable. I pointed out that there was no way any flame could come near the stage and promised faithfully that the set would come down the following day. To my enormous relief I got away with it.

Baxter's association with the Globe was not only as a playwright. In 1965 and 1968 we put out our first little publications about the theatre; I wrote the first (and solicited advertisements for both) and Jimmy (as we generally called him) provided the text for the second one. To our surprise we had requests from libraries all round the country on the strength of the Baxter contribution. James also gave several poetry readings, including the first airing of the now famous 'A Small Ode on Mixed Flatting', which was written in response to Otago University's prohibition of the practice, and printed as a broadsheet on Patric's recommendation, to the delight of the students.

As well as a significant writer, Baxter was a many-faceted personality. No matter what his critics may say, he cared greatly about his wife and two children, and really tried to be of help to young people. I had known him to sit with young people for an hour or so allowing them to pour out their problems. One day when Christopher was in hospital and I couldn't visit him because I had a children's production in the theatre, and Patric decided he was too busy, James was his only visitor. He took him a comic and an apple.

On one occasion James actually took part in a Globe production. I will not say he acted, because he simply sat on the stage and delivered his lines in his own persona, not difficult as he admitted, since he was cast as the drunken doctor in *The Cherry Orchard*. However, apart from being a wonderful drawcard for audiences, Patric felt that James would benefit from being in a great play, and I was particularly pleased that someone other than Patric would play the part. I felt he had more than enough to do directing a Chekhov play, which needs such careful orchestration.

After the first rehearsal I found a little note in the letterbox to say that James had decided he had not the time to be in the play. To me this was ironic. Patric was giving hours of his time to James's work, and whereas amateur companies producing new New Zealand plays could apply for subsidies from the New Zealand Theatre Federation, and possibly have a paid director as well, we were not considered eligible for this assistance as we were *professionals*. The only guaranteed financial help we had was the Arts Council's £200 a year for royalties and of this James regularly received his share.

I knew James would have no idea what his withdrawal would mean to Patric, but I certainly did, and decided to take action. I was not sure of the address but I called a taxi, enquired at various places, and ultimately found him. With a little gentle persuasion he agreed to play the part. He was very nervous about learning lines, so carefully pasted the words into a newspaper which he had, quite legitimately, on the stage.

In this production of *The Cherry Orchard* Fred Kersh played the elderly servant Fiers. Ever since seeing the play in London when he was very young, he had wanted the part. He asked if he could have it the first time we did the play, but Patric told him, 'You only play Fiers when you are too old for anything else, and I want you for Vershinin.'

But now he was retiring from performance in the theatre. Fred had given so much to the Globe as an actor, backstage worker, member of the audience and the Friends committee, but he obviously felt it was worth it. He said to me recently:

Dunedin owes a tremendous debt of gratitude to the Careys – they opened up the world of great theatre. They eschewed the double-door, floral-hat romantic and comic plays well established in London's West End, and gave us Strindberg, Ionesco, Lorca, Ibsen, Tennessee Williams, Albee, the Greeks and Chekhov ...

Fred was not a Baxter fan – but many of our younger patrons would have put Baxter well at the top of the list.

Early the following year there was a return Baxter season at the Globe. In June 1973 four of the plays were presented in Wellington. Patric directed *The Temptations of Oedipus*, with Judith Fyfe as Antigone; Philip Mann chose *The Devil and Mr Mulcahy*, Anthony Groser *The Band Rotunda*, and Judith Dale *The Sore-Footed Man*.

Colin McCahon created a symbolic set to serve them all. Wellington audiences were very different from ours – they did not have the background of Greek drama, and were perhaps less disposed towards

Baxter. Whatever the reason the venture was far from being a success.

These four plays – *The Band Rotunda*, *The Devil and Mr Mulcahy*, *The Sore-Footed Man* and *The Temptations of Oedipus* – were published by Heinemann in 1974 and in 1981 the *Collected Plays* of James K. Baxter was published by Oxford University Press. Several have had productions since, but the importance of this period did not lie in the plays themselves. Patric would be the first to admit that James had not totally grasped the technique of writing effectively for the theatre, but the response of the younger generation showed New Zealand dramatists that there was a place for them in our theatres, particularly if they could ally themselves with a good director.

Others – Peter Harcourt, Bruce Mason, David Carnegie, Frank McKay, and Wilhelmina Drummond – have written at length about this era, and there is also a short educational film. I leave further comment to them.

CHAPTER XI

Ebb and Flow

More Baxter – Beckett – Shakespeare

ૐ

Right in the middle of the Baxter season was a production of Bernard Shaw's political comedy, *The Apple Cart,* a play that is rarely produced in spite of present preoccupation with the future of the monarchy. In it, the king of England is forced to abdicate because of his radical ideas, only to announce that he will stand for President. A highlight in Patric's production was Ray Stone, playing King Magnus. Ray's comment in the *Globe* anniversary booklet was:

> Patric helped insights to come by his alertness and his modest and relaxed capacity for sensitizing his often unpromising amateur actors. And how admirable was Patric's respect for good English in his Shaw productions! Dramatic 'business' was never called on to 'sell' text which didn't need 'selling'. I remember gratefully his encouragement simply to present King Magnus's fourteen-minute speech in 'The Apple Cart' without hurry or apology. Shaw didn't need any help other than getting out of his way …

In this case, though, Shaw was helped greatly by Dr Ray Stone's intelligence and beautiful speaking voice.

Els Noordhof designed the costumes all in black-and-white. Being futuristic, the play offered plenty of scope for a creative artist. I particularly remember the black velvet gown edged with feathers worn by Pamela Pow and the white linen suit made for Hal Smith, with a handpainted pattern all over the jacket.

During this production we had one of our many 'leaking-roof' dramas. I had invited the newly arrived Vice-Chancellor of Otago University and so hoped that all would go particularly well. Towards the interval heavy rain set in. As the play progressed I watched with trepidation as the cardboard ceiling under the tarras began to sag. Two seconds after the actors made their exit, the weight of the water dislodged the cardboard and water poured all over the stage. A maid – in costume – made an unrehearsed appearance armed with mop and bucket.

Following the return season of Baxter plays we did our second production of Beckett's *Endgame*. We had a very different cast and were now in a position to take increasing liberties with our audience. In the newsletter announcing *Endgame*, Patric wrote:

If you enjoyed *Endgame* the first time, you will certainly want to see it again. If you disliked it, remember you are now seven times more theatrically mature; our actors are ninety-seven plays more experienced, and the world is seven years more ridiculous.

There are certainly some happy, if ridiculous, memories of this production. The old couple in the dustbins were none other than Ian and Judy Ralston, the two major roles being played by Ern Joyce, who was in our original production of *Waiting for Godot*, and Clive Bayliss, who did every possible job in our theatre and who has since become a veteran video and film editor.

Endgame appealed enormously to ten-year-old Belinda. After Sunday afternoon rehearsals and Saturday night performances she and Clive would mount the ladders on the stage and go through whole scenes of the play together. She wrote a beautiful letter to Samuel Beckett, which spoke of the 'caves of people's minds'. After adding a note about her age I duly sent it off care of the publishers, even though the author had a reputation for never answering letters. Some weeks later Belinda received a copy of Beckett's latest publication, *Cascando*, with a little handwritten note from the great man on the title page.

Whereas for most societies one Shakespearean production would be a major event, in 1968 we staged two – *Twelfth Night* directed by Patric and *The Winter's Tale* by Hal Smith. Each ran from Tuesday to Sunday of alternate weeks for a six-week season. In all there were no less than one hundred people involved. Bill Mackay, who played Autolycus in *The Winter's Tale* and Feste in *Twelfth Night*, was the only actor to be in both productions.

It was in *Twelfth Night* that Simon O'Connor made his debut at the Globe, as one of the young men at Orsino's court. The other was John Reid, an experienced actor, who later worked at the Fortune Theatre, produced plays, conducted children's classes at the Globe, and for some time was art critic for the *Otago Daily Times*. The imbalance between the two – the shy newcomer contrasted with the taller, experienced actor – was the one weak spot in an otherwise beautiful production. Simon, of course, went on to greater things in the theatre, whereas John has recently left the arts world in favour of business.

Although Patric wanted to stress its dark side, *Twelfth Night* was a happy production. A particular joy for me was seeing Marilyn Parker's portrayal of Olivia. Having worked hard in my classes for years, appeared in a series of unrewarding roles, and done endless jobs backstage she emerged like a beautiful butterfly in a performance that would have graced any stage.

For *Twelfth Night* Rodney Kennedy excelled himself with the costumes, based on Watteau paintings. In spite of their disparate sizes Sandra Burt as Viola and Peter Clare as Sebastian made credible twins. Their colouring and features were quite similar and they were helped by their matching grey-green satin costumes, beautifully made by Pamela Pow.

Rodney designed fanciful hats and shoes, many of which he made himself, but the costumes were, as usual, made by my band of helpers on a minimal budget. I was very proud of Feste's costume, which was nothing more than the full-circle skirt of a satin wedding gown with a ruff and one of Rodney's wonderful hats. Els Noordhof did a beautiful painting of Bill wearing it, which she later gave to Patric.

Marilyn Parker speaks with affection of the ice-blue gown she wore, made from several evening dresses. It was very heavy but that did not worry her and she looked really beautiful in Rodney's adorable little veiled hat. But she also remembers one awful moment when she spilt tea down the front of her dress: 'We panicked, but we sponged and ironed it in time to save ourselves from Rodney's wrath.' It is surprising that she escaped mine as well, for eating or drinking in costume without a dressing gown was forbidden in the theatre.

When Hal Smith was planning *The Winter's Tale*, he insisted that I play Amelia. I was delighted, but hesitant to commit myself when there were so many costumes involved. However, Hal assured me that his wife, artist Els Noordhof, would take care of the wardrobe. That did not, of course, mean that I would be totally free of responsibility because no one else knew where things lived, whereas I could account for the tiniest piece of jewellery or trim.

A few days before opening night one of Hal's cast fell ill, and Hal took over the part. Under these circumstances I was distressed to find him in the theatre on his own, the night before we opened, making last minute adjustments to the set. We both worked till one o'clock in the morning. Tiredness does nothing for the memory, and I can only hope the first night audience were not too familiar with the play for I rewrote line after line.

Such situations enhanced my desire to see the Globe become

professional or alternatively to have the opportunity to work with professionals elsewhere. Patric, on the other hand, was concerned only with producing the plays he wanted to do and he feared that if we turned professional he would have to give greater consideration to the box office. Though it was politic to keep introducing new actors he was happiest working with the people he knew and he contrived to have a hard core of them in each production.

Lack of money and failing energy did not seem to worry him. His casts still worshipped him and, generally speaking, he treated them with the utmost consideration, but at times I found him quite unreasonable. For instance, even though I had at least three perfectly capable young girls longing for good parts, he insisted on Maureen Edwards playing three major roles in a row. The third was the demanding role of the young girl in *The Master Builder*, one of Ibsen's later and most powerful plays, about a middle-aged man who falls to his death as the result of the infatuation of a young girl in search of a hero. Geoffrey Jowett gave a memorable performance in the title role.

It is true that Maureen was a particularly fine actress, but she was at teachers' college, had her own drama class at the Globe, and was preparing for her LTCL examination. Into the bargain she developed flu. Little wonder that at one Sunday afternoon rehearsal I found her sitting on the steps of the foyer in tears. I could do little more than ask Patric to excuse her from the rehearsal, but Maureen plodded on and gave her usual fine performance. Ten days after the season ended, she sat and passed her speech examination with a reasonably good mark.

Fortunately, Maureen's enthusiasm for working at the Globe was in no way impaired. Somewhere along the line Patric had promised her that one day she should play the title role in *The Duchess of Malfi*. By the time our second production of the play was scheduled (in 1968) Maureen had left Dunedin for the North Island, but she was happy to return for the season.

Philip Smithells, at last retired from the School of Physical Education but recovering from a stroke, was entrusted with the huge role of the Duke. Ian Fraser – journalist, broadcaster, erstwhile member of the Queen Elizabeth II Arts Council, chairman of public relations company Consultus, commissioner-general of the Brisbane and Seville Expo, and now manager of the New Zealand Symphony Orchestra – was our Bosola. Recently he recalled that, fine actor though Philip was, he was inclined to get words mixed up, creating an extra challenge for the other actors. Iain Lonie was cast as the Duchess's other brother, the cardinal, and gave a terrifying performance of unbalanced evil. Unfortunately, he was unavailable the following year for the second season and Patric played his part. In this revival, Sandra Burt took over the role of the Duchess, giving it a totally different interpretation.

This production was traumatic for me as well. Catherine Sinton, a most talented young woman, was in charge of the costumes. Patric claimed he had very definite ideas about colours and style but failed to advise us till it meant a last minute rush. This was disastrous for Catherine, who was seriously asthmatic and needed to be sheltered from pressure. Sadly, she died a few months later.

There is, however, a happier story. One lovely sunny morning I was actually taking a little time out to join some friends on the steps by the front entrance of the garden, just talking and having a pleasant time. Rehearsals for *The Duchess* were going well and we had only one small worry. We needed one more man to help carry the coffin after the Duchess's death.

Simon O'Connor was with us as well as a young friend of his, a personable young man with an interest in acting. Needless to say I captured him at once as a coffin bearer and a madman. He enjoyed being on the boards but his interest in singing led him to join the Dunedin Opera Company, with whom he soon found his feet as well as his voice. It was a move that changed his life, for he has become an international tenor. His name is Patrick Power.

The plays of Edward Albee were always significant for us. We had already done *The American Dream* with John Grigor (a brilliant medical student) in the lead, *Who's Afraid of Virginia Woolf?* (which I have already mentioned) and *Tiny Alice*, a dark, mysterious play which once again featured Eve Durning and Richard Hlavac. I cannot resist including Richard's comments from the anniversary booklet:

> At the end of 'Tiny Alice', I had an extremely long monologue (about 20 minutes) after I had been shot, during which I had to gasp, crawl around the stage, throw open my jacket to reveal a particularly nasty gunshot wound (concocted from nail polish) and then die … The performance must have been pretty moving because one night the lady sitting next to Jackie [Richard's wife] in the audience, threw up in her handbag.

Patric's fanatical expectations of actors were again apparent when we did Albee's *A Delicate Balance* in 1969. He invited his long-time friend Natalie Dolamore to play the lead. Natalie lived in Gore and, along with her parents, had billeted Patric on several occasions when he was working for the Repertory Society there. I had also enjoyed their hospitality and Natalie stayed with us from time to time. Natalie lacked confidence but was a competent actress with a lovely speaking voice and she was prepared to make the two-and-a-half hour journey to Dunedin three times a week. When rehearsals were well underway it was discovered that the playing dates clashed with Library Week, and she was the chief librarian.

For some unknown reason Patric would not change our schedule, believing till the end that Natalie would sacrifice her career in favour of the Globe. Inevitably, the combination of nerves and exhaustion played havoc with her memory. I was prompting on the first night and my heart went out to her. She struggled through as best she could, her own charm compensating to some extent for her dependence on the prompt. She continued to do her arduous day's work and travel to Dunedin in the evening, giving an ever-improving performance for the rest of the season.

But there were also times when Patric's handling of people impressed me greatly – for instance when speech and drama tutor Mary Hopewell brought her teachers' college students to watch a rehearsal (something she did annually) and one of our actors was late. We sat around and talked, trying to entertain our visitors till the young man arrived – obviously drunk. When he stumbled into the theatre, there was a little pause and then Patric said very calmly, 'I'm sorry, people, there will be no rehearsal tonight. I do not tolerate drunkenness in my theatre!' He asked me to make supper for our cast and guests. Embarrassing though it was, the young people declared it had been a valuable lesson.

Certainly there were plenty of good parties at the Globe and Patric was known for his generous pre-dinner and luncheon martinis. On Saturdays when there was a show on, food and drinks would arrive as if by magic and, when the set was suitable, Patric would put on some music and we would dance. I was passionately fond of dancing but Patric claimed he had two left feet and was tone deaf. Nothing could have been further from the truth, but like Noel Coward's Nina from Argentina 'he resolutely wouldn't dance'.

The partying we enjoyed the most was when a few stragglers who had perhaps helped to do a little clearing up would assemble round our breakfast-room table with a bottle, and maybe a loaf of bread and some cheese. Particularly when Rodney Kennedy was there, stories and laughter would flow non-stop for hours.

Alcohol had its place but not in the theatre during or before 'working hours'. When Patric was involved in a production he would never drink after five o'clock. Yet on one occasion when he was playing a long and arduous part – one of the few he performed other than as a stand-in for someone else – he had a bilious attack which could well have been caused by exhaustion. Having struggled to the end of the play without any obvious signs of the problem, he retired upstairs and collapsed onto the bed. Independent as he usually was, he allowed Christopher to remove his jackboots but fell asleep in his uniform. Imagine his chagrin when it was suggested that he been drinking!

Whereas in the past Patric and I had been a great working team, communication was now becoming increasingly difficult. There were times when I could have thrown the whole enterprise away, but with so much on the plus side I felt things just had to come right one day.

We were becoming known not only in New Zealand but overseas as well. In the early days an article written by Anne de Roo had appeared in the *New Yorker*, and we were mentioned in the 1967 edition of the *Oxford Companion to the Theatre*. Simon O'Connor had heard about us in Tonga, and John Hunter while in Ghana.

We had several visitors from the United States, some with introductions from John Casserley who had gone back there to lecture in a private university. It was flattering I suppose, but these young visitors seemed to think we had nothing to do but sit around and talk to them. So I evolved the scheme that if they had conducted, or even taken part in, a drama course, they should share their knowledge with my students – anything to bring in fresh ideas. The greatest drawback of working in Dunedin was the lack of outside stimulus, so much so that on one occasion I went to Wellington to a meeting of Theatre Federation to plead on behalf of the young people in the South. They agreed to send a tutor for a weekend school, but to our great disappointment, made it a school for directors, which was of limited interest to my keen young actors. Certainly we were always on the lookout for directors, but they needed to be experienced.

We also needed fresh faces and new angles for press releases. Then one day out of the blue came a letter from Anne Hill, an American drama graduate enquiring about working in our theatre. She was prepared to come all the way to New Zealand to take part in the kind of play we did at the Globe. I sent her our first two little publications about the theatre and explained that we could not offer her a salary.

However, after considerable correspondence, she decided she would try to get a teaching job and come anyway. I was delighted and invited her to stay with us on arrival.

She was a sensitive girl, having been very sheltered, and was quite unable to cope with Patric's acerbic wit and provocative arguments, especially when it came to her favourite dramatist, Chekhov. Nevertheless she worked happily with me in the studio until, unable to find anything suitable locally, she took a position teaching English and drama at the polytechnic in Invercargill. Before she left, in order that she should have at least one show at the Globe to her credit, I arranged a programme for her with Heather Eggleton who was then working for Dunedin television. They performed their favourite scenes in our most attractive costumes and gave us a very enjoyable programme.

Though Anne was desperately lonely in Invercargill at first, it was not too long before she met a nice young man who asked her to marry him. They had an Edwardian wedding with the reception at the Globe. Patric was asked to give the bride away. He appeared resplendent in frock coat, coloured waistcoat, top hat, and spats, carrying his silver-topped cane. He enjoyed dressing up and was grateful not to have to wear a suit as he no longer had one that fitted him.

Anne's was not the only wedding to be held at the Globe. Barbara (formerly Casserley) and Peter Robinson celebrated their nuptials in the theatre. Since the Globe was an unconsecrated building, the ceremony was to take place in the garden but it rained. At a moment's notice Patric created a simple little altar by throwing a piece of velvet over a couple of boxes, with a large candle and a rose on top.

It was an Elizabethan wedding. The bride and groom each made their own costumes and all the guests dressed appropriately – largely from the Globe wardrobe. The banquet was set out on trestle tables and featured a boar's head, a haggis, large round loaves of bread made especially by a local baker, a haunch of beef, and a cane cornucopia overflowing with fruit.

The next part of our story seems to be a matter of oscillating fate and ironies. For instance, I was actually grateful for a massive dose of 'flu which kept me in bed for several days. Patric and the children, who were rarely forthcoming with any help in the house, seemed to thoroughly enjoy cooking excellent dinners – totally unsuitable for an invalid, but appreciated nevertheless.

During this time I was able to read some plays and of these had the opportunity to direct Bernard Shaw's *The Simpleton of the Unexpected Isles* at St Hilda's and *Too True to be Good* at the Globe. The latter is a long difficult play but there were good parts for several of my students including Helen O'Grady and Simon O'Connor, who played the leads. As well I was very much in sympathy with the anti-war theme. It was an ambitious project for me and fitting a hermit's shrine and a tent onto our stage were among the least of my problems.

Following the improved reception of *Endgame* it was not surprising that Patric chose to do a second production of *Waiting for Godot*. This time the cast consisted of Geoffrey Jowett and Basil James, a popular Dunedin character who had not acted for us before. The other two, Ern Joyce (Pozzo in both productions) and Clive Bayliss (Lucky), were well known to our audiences. Between them this cast found symbols and meanings even Patric had not discovered, making rehearsals a sheer delight for all concerned.

Let Geoffrey Jowett recount an amusing episode:

> I thought (perhaps mistakenly) that it was as a psychiatrist and a statistician that Basil James and I were deemed suitable to utter deep but random lines stuffed with symbols while dressed as a pair of dirty tramps ...

Patric assured us that deliberate acting was undesirable; that the play and the actors' thinking about it would evolve together with minimal prods from him as a very non-directive producer. Perhaps this explains some spurious but plausible Beckett dialogue at one performance:

> Didi (James): You're in the wrong act!
> Gogo (Jowett): True. What shall we do?
> Didi: We'll have have to go back! But how?
> Gogo: To the tree.
> Didi: Yes, let's go back to the tree ...
>
> (At this point blind Pozzo, Joyce and Lucky, waiting for Godot in the wings, were virtually catapulted on stage by the ever-vigilant Patric, thus somewhat prematurely catching Gogo unequipped for kicking Lucky.)
>
> Pozzo: Whaaat's happening?
> Didi: (describing the state of affairs) My friend is putting on his boots.
>
> (Did the audience notice? We never heard.)

One member did. I was sitting in the back row, knew something was amiss and flew backstage to assist a fairly inexperienced prompt. Beckett's dialogue consists of very short lines that don't always seem to follow sequentially, so it is extremely easy to get them out of place. Actors frequently leave out a piece of dialogue, but these two had the audacity, or should I say courage, to put a whole scene back and join it up successfully. Questioned after the performance Basil James explained to me, 'My wife's in the audience tonight. That was a good bit and I didn't want her to miss it.'

This production drew full houses every night – not surprising since it was in the university stage one English syllabus. No actor or manager could fail to be elated to have the theatre full but, typical of the Carey fortunes, our keen young supporters had sold practically every seat to students at cheap rates, leaving little room for those paying the proper price! The result was that, as usual, we made very little money.

The best cash flow of 1969 came from an unexpected quarter. Now that our population mix was becoming diversified, we had the idea of staging an International Concert. With the assistance of our good supporter Miss Rewa Begg MBE, the doyenne of the YWCA, we put together an exciting programme of dance and music with Peggy Durrant representing the Kiwis with an original poem. A bus load came from Invercargill and the young Indian dancer was so popular that we later had her give us a solo performance accompanied solely by drummers. Both occasions were tremendously exciting and the full-house notice went up on both occasions.

Since Patric was teaching not only at Knox College but also one afternoon a week at the seminary in Mosgiel, we were extremely fortunate to have several guest productions including Ian and Judy Ralston in Wesker's two-hander *The Four Seasons,* in which Judy, looking wonderful in a white fur coat and hat, with white boots, had to sustain a whole act in total silence while Ian delivered the dialogue solo.

There was also Pamela Pow's delightful production of *Shelley – or the Idealist,* and a double bill – *Andorra* (Max Frisch) and *Woyzeck* (Georg Büchner) by the German department of the university and *The Spirit and the Flesh, Dramatic Monologues* selected from Robert Browning's *Dramatis Personae* and directed by Hal Smith. Browning had always been a favourite poet of mine. I loved his sense of drama. Had he lived at a time when serious theatre was in vogue I am sure he would have been a wonderful playwright.

Hal assembled a strong cast including himself, Ray Stone, Phillip Gaze, Alistair Douglas, Brent Southgate and Ian Fraser, who wrote and delivered the introduction and framework. I was quite envious of Hal but it worked in my favour for I was able to enjoy Browning's work without the responsibility and angst, and later I directed a short version with some of the lighter material included for the university schools tour. As well I had the privilege of accompanying a group from Hal's production when they were invited to entertain at a University Women's end-of-year dinner. The banquet was more lavish than anything I had ever seen but, just as I was about to indulge myself, I was advised that I would have to introduce the programme. I could still appreciate the visual delights of the meal but the shock had removed all the pleasure of eating.

As soon as his teaching year finished Patric retired to our holiday home – a wonderful escape hatch on the shores of Lake Mahinerangi I had managed to purchase at a ridiculously low price, thanks to a small family legacy. It was freezing cold in winter, but not too bad in summer, enabling us to swim and fish and, hopefully, to relax – a great place to heal frayed nerves and find a little peace and quiet.

I was grateful that Patric had plenty of time to enjoy the healing air of Mahinerangi. However, I was still busy with pupils – and there was the Christmas revue Shirley Mackenzie and I wrote and presented, *Black Champagne*, which included blatant sideswipes at the Arts Council.

This left me pretty frayed and I looked forward eagerly to spending a quiet time just with family. But Patric had invited the cast of *A Sleep of Prisoners* (Christopher Fry) to begin rehearsals at the lake in the latter part of the holidays. Although I liked the idea of the place being used as widely as possible, this meant not only the cast but wives and children as well, and at one stage I found myself providing for no less than fifteen people. We were fifteen kilometres from the nearest store and had no car!

Furthermore Patric invited me to play Lady Elizabeth, the mother, in T.S. Eliot's *The Family Reunion*. I questioned my ability to learn this difficult role, but he simply said, 'Who else?' So I began studying the play during the holidays and of course accepted the challenge.

CHAPTER XII

A Change of Course

The Globe is sold to the Friends

৯

If Patric and I were exhausted and disillusioned as a result of our foolhardy attempts to establish theatre in the Victorian city of Dunedin, we were not the only ones. In 1969 the Southern Trust still had the backing of the Arts Council but, by-passing Bernard Esquilant and Bill Menlove, it had engaged Warwick Slyfield, whose experience had been largely in musical comedy, as artistic director. One would have expected it to be a temporary arrangement, but, in spite of all their hard work and enthusiasm, Bernard and Bill were never to hold the reins again.

Although the Southern Players were no longer offering training for the theatre, they still appreciated its value and, to my surprise and delight they asked us if we would train actors for the Playhouse. The Arts Council had consistently implied that Dunedin's problems arose from lack of co-operation between groups but we were only too pleased to throw in our lot with our erstwhile partners and rivals, as long as the money could be appropriately apportioned. We all felt highly optimistic, but once again the Arts Council refused to co-operate. Little wonder that soon afterwards Bernard and Bill retired from the theatre for ever.

After a short time Warwick Slyfield took an engagement with the Mercury Theatre in Auckland and in a last desperate bid to retrieve the Southern Players, the Trust advertised for a director overseas. They engaged David Phethean, a charming Englishman with excellent credentials.

After a good start with a successful comedy, David was required to produce Shakespeare's *Macbeth,* which was, of course, in the secondary school syllabus. Due to various circumstances he found himself without a cast. In desperation he telephoned me. (It was ironic that we had so recently staged two Shakespeare plays concurrently.) I recommended several very young players but was exercised to think of anyone mature enough for the leads.

It so happened that Simon O'Connor was leaving Dunedin the following morning to try his luck up North. Since Simon had the experience and the intelligence for the part, David was prepared to have a very young Macbeth. I had no idea where Simon was living, but after about a dozen phone calls managed to track him down. He auditioned and was accepted, and on my suggestion Heather Eggleton played opposite him. David settled for a cast young enough to support the leads. Several of my teenage students were included. He set the play in the nineteenth century and we helped with costumes and properties.

Our help was obviously appreciated for David did everything he could to assist when I visited England in 1974. He was then artistic director of the highly respected Bristol Old Vic Company.

Unfortunately for *Macbeth* the local papers were far from kind, comparing it unfavourably with Shakespearean productions at the Globe. Apart from school parties, audiences were limited and the Arts Council withdrew their support. The Southern Trust had been given a $20,000 grant, but David's fare and salary used two-thirds of this.

By 1971 the Southern Players had disappeared, leaving a legacy of the Playhouse to the Repertory Society. Ironically Patric had recommended it to them as a permanent home many years before.

Having the field to ourselves should have solved all our problems, but alas it was too late. Patric and I were tired – overworked, underpaid, our health deteriorating and relations between us strained to say the least. For most of his life Patric had enjoyed phenomenally good health and continued to work himself to the limit, but having had several 'burnouts' I tried always to keep a little bit in reserve. The children were being neglected and I could see no light at the end of the tunnel.

The Arts Council had at last understood the wisdom of companies having their own premises, and when they came to see us towards the end of 1969 it was my impression that they would help us as far as possible – even with providing extra toilets so that we could become a public theatre. This time it was Patric who was unco-operative.

The principal Arts Council argument was that our theatre was on private property. Colin Durning, then chairman of the Friends of the Globe Theatre, Ian Ralston and Patric had long sessions working out policy and strategies from which, to my chagrin, I found myself largely excluded.

Then one day Patric came to me full of excitement over a wonderful idea of which Ian and Colin had approved. If Arts Council money

Above: Cover for programme of Baxter's The Band Rotunda, *1968, and ensuing productions. The photograph shows Jim Wright as the Herald in* Marat/Sade *by Weiss, performed at the Globe in the previous year.*
Below: Baxter's play The Devil and Mr Mulcahy, *1967, one of the seven Baxter plays premiered by the Globe. Left to right: Ian Ralston, Peggy Durrant, Richard Mercier and Ian Hudson.*

Above: Patric in the garden. The theatre can be seen to the left of the house, the magnolia tree is to the right, 1968.
Below: Maureen Edwards as the Duchess and Iain Lonie as the Cardinal in a rehearsal of The Duchess of Malfi, *by Webster, 1968.*

Above left to right: Marilyn Parker, Sandra Burt and Helen O'Grady in
Shakespeare's Twelfth Night, *1968.*
Below: Shakespeare's The Winter's Tale, *1968. Left: Musicians perform on the*
tarras, and right: 'Exit, pursued by a bear', Frank Grayson as the bear, Les Coxhead
as Antigonus.

Above: The Children of the Globe Theatre in The Pied Piper, *a children's opera, by Browning, adapted by Moira Fleming, produced for television in 1969.*
Left: Ray Stone as Creon in Baxter's play The Temptations of Oedipus, *1970.*

could not be available to private property, then why not sell the house and theatre to the Friends with the proviso that we could continue to live in our home at a peppercorn rent?

I was so grateful for anything that might save us from the 'no-win' situation we were in, that I for one did not look much further ahead, and agreed to the proposal. Surely Patric would receive a salary and we could at last have a little family life. I also believed it would mean that the Globe would ultimately become truly professional.

The great scheme was put into action. Debentures were raised; the cottage next door that had belonged to the Misses Kaye was purchased for the wardrobe, the fire chief having ordered it peremptorily from its home under the raked section of the auditorium. Patric at last had an office, a luxury neither of us had enjoyed in all those years. Small though the rooms in the cottage were, they gave us space for rehearsals and meetings. (We had been known to have as many as five activities happening simultaneously in the house, with me conducting a drama class or a rehearsal in our bedroom.)

A legal document was duly drawn up, the salient points being:

1. THE Society agrees to grant a tenancy of the residence situated at 104 London Street to the tenants:

2. THE initial term shall be for a period of 3 years with a right of renewal for a further 5 years and with rights of further renewal.

3. THE initial rental shall be the sum of $2.00 per week but this rental shall at the discretion of the Society be increased up to a maximum of $10 per week based on $1.00 per week for every additional $100.00 of salary above the present minimum salary hereby agreed to be paid.

(This rental may sound ridiculous, but it must be understood that the purchase was not to be at market value but simply *what the society could afford.* And this was $12,000 for an eighth-of-an-acre section in a most desirable position overlooking the city, plus the house, the theatre, and the assets.)

Other relevant clauses were:

(b) FOR the initial period a guaranteed minimum income of five hundred dollars per annum shall be payable by the Society to the Director and it is hereby declared as being understood between the parties that this initial minimum salary has been fixed on a tentative basis only and after an initial period shall be subject to review by way of increase having regard to the income produced and general and specific donations and financial assistance made available to the Society.

(Everyone was confident the Arts Council would come to the party, but it transpired that the highest annual salary Patric received was $15,000.)

(f) THE proceeds of all activities in the form of the productions and exhibitions or other artistic activities shall be payable to the Society which may in its discretion allocate to the Director such percentage or percentages as it may deem just and equitable.

INSOFAR as the Wardrobe of the Globe Theatre is concerned the following conditions shall apply:–

(a) THE said Rosalie Louise Carey shall have full access to the wardrobe at all times and be generally responsible for its maintenance with a right to call on the Society for assistance where necessary and shall also have the right at any time to hire out any costumes which are not being currently used in any production staged by the Society and it is agreed by and between the parties that any income from the hire of costumes shall be divided on the basis that the Society shall receive 40% and the said Rosalie Louise Carey 60% thereof.

The wardrobe had been very important to me and I looked upon it as my personal domain. Costume hire made a considerable contribution to my income. Having started with nothing, I had accumulated approximately eight hundred costumes, to say nothing of usable material and accessories. Among them were many genuine period costumes dating back to the 1880s.

Other details in the document stated that at last Patric and I were no longer responsible for bookings, the newsletter, or the maintenance and cleaning of the theatre. The Friends would take care of financial matters and the upkeep of the buildings and garden, but Patric was to continue having complete artistic freedom.

It was also agreed that I should be:

entitled to operate as a separate entity the Theatre School and to this end [she shall] have the free use of the Theatre for teaching provided that in respect of electricity and heating charges she shall bear a just fair and equitable proportion of these items such proportion to be assessed by consultation between the Society and the said Rosalie Louise Carey ...

Grandiose plans were announced for the future, including taking productions elsewhere and bringing others to Dunedin. There would be four guest productions at the Globe; Patric would remain for one more year after which the Friends would advertise for a new director. Improvements would be made to the building, and an open-air theatre established in the cottage garden.

To celebrate the purchase of the cottage my students and I begged and borrowed enough furniture and chattels to set it up as it might have been before the turn of the century, opened it to the public for a whole weekend and, dressed in period costumes, served tea as required. It was an interesting experience for us all.

The big event of early 1970 was the production of *The Temptations of Oedipus*. Since it was Baxter's last play it seemed appropriate that it should be Patric's final one before handing over the reins – or some of them. Bookings flooded in and I had visions of a real financial success. But Patric chose to make it the first production for the new organisation, so the takings went to the Friends!

As well as Hotere's water-colours, paintings by Jeffrey Harris were exhibited. Ralph and Michael Smither (past and current Frances Hodgkins Fellows) had 'discovered' Jeffrey. They provided him with studio space and arranged his first exhibition at the Museum Art Gallery. At a later exhibition I heard him described as one of our leading painters.

Inspired by watching a rehearsal of *Oedipus*, Jeffrey did a very large painting based on the play. It consisted of a series of scenes with captions, one of which read, 'I fuck my mother!' The late Colin McDonald, who had just taken over the chairmanship from Colin Durning, and several of the Friends' committee were deeply offended by the painting. A meeting was called and Patric summoned. Patric saw this as an ominous challenge to his artistic autonomy but, sincere in his wish for the new arrangement to succeed, he suggested a compromise. The painting would not be on public view, but hung in the dressing room for the benefit of broad-minded patrons.

The first guest production after that was in the capable hands of Ian Ralston. It was a small-cast version of *American Hurrah* featuring Ian Fraser, Nevan Rowe, and Derek Payne. Derek was front man for television's *Town and Around,* and was very popular with Dunedin audiences in tandem with the now famous Dave McPhail. Both appeared later in Terry Bryan's production of John Antrobus's *You'll Come to Love Your Sperm Test.*

Mid-year Patric directed Strindberg's *Easter.* I had so much wanted to do it earlier with Peggy Jowett and Richard Mercier, but now Richard was no longer available, and though we had Peggy we were short of a young girl to play the older sister. Patric left the search entirely to me. I finally settled for a student I had seen in a German play at the Globe, and recommended Kathleen Dawson for the role of the mother. Kathleen is a very talented but unconfident performer and Patric was not really compatible with either of these two women. He did, however, have Geoffrey Jowett who recalls:

> 10 nerve-racking one-minute appearances uniformly spread through the play *Easter*, taken on because 'You'll be bringing Peggy to rehearsal and picking her up afterwards anyway', have involved us and our families in very worthwhile experiences in plays which were far more interesting than we ever imagined plays could be …

It was wonderful to be relieved of at least some of the pressures. Even so by the end of the winter, following demanding productions of *The Family Reunion* and *Uncle Vanya*, Patric's health was becoming a real concern. I had complained enough about being perpetually tired myself but now that seemed unimportant. As I saw it, the theatre and the family were utterly dependent on him, even though at times I had coped on my own for weeks on end.

Eventually, I took the initiative and told Patric I would take responsibility for the next production. I would somehow find a way of giving him a break, even if I had to do a solo strip-tease, for I feared he might 'break' in a more serious manner. He accepted my offer graciously.

There had been no time for me to read plays, so I had no idea how to fill the slot. However, some years before I had read Janet Frame's *A State of Siege* and envisaged it as a radio play. When I mentioned this to Bill Austin, head of Radio New Zealand's drama department, he suggested I should first adapt it for the stage. Needless to say I had given the idea little more thought. But now, quite suddenly a format flashed into my mind and I made a snap decision.

In the August holidays I gathered up my portable typewriter and a few supplies, and with Christopher to keep me company took a taxi to Lake Mahinerangi. It was already snowing when we left and a storm raged for the four days we were there. A roaring gale chased snow flakes horizontally past the windows – fitting atmosphere for the drama I was writing, for wind and rain pound the house where Malfred Signal spent her first, and last, night alone.

There was no proper heating at our holiday home (the range wouldn't work because the chimney was blocked), so it was no fun sitting at a typewriter. However, I wrote non-stop and came back to town with a short play, which I thought could be preceded by music and/or poetry.

Janet Frame was the Burns Fellow at Otago University that year and it was arranged that I should read my dramatisation to her and Ian and Judy Ralston. (There were no copying machines available to us in those days so I gave a solo reading.) The reaction was one of enthusiasm.

Ian had just recovered from a bout of pneumonia which had interrupted the season of *Uncle Vanya* in which he was playing the major role of Astrov, the doctor, but to my surprise and delight he offered to direct *A State of Siege.*

Though I had not imagined myself doing so, Janet and the Ralstons all decided I should play Malfred Signal, who is on stage throughout, and talking most of the time. Ian made some excellent suggestions. We introduced more material from the book by way of recorded voices, so that the play ran for one hour twenty minutes. The intensity of the drama was such that there was no need for a supporting programme.

Typically, Patric could not rest but offered to built the set. He created the exterior of 'the white house on the hill' in polystyrene, cut away to reveal the interior. It was complete with red corrugated iron roof (made from cardboard) and little details like a drainpipe in one corner. Above, black plastic with jagged slits revealed the lightning in the storm scene. Shirley Mackenzie said recently that it was the finest set she has ever seen.

I rejoiced to be back on the boards though I missed the cameraderie of a normal show. Other parts were very small and Ian chose to use fairly inexperienced actors, two of whom I didn't know at all.

But I loved repeating Janet's rich colourful words in phrases like 'giant patriarchal pohutukawa dipping their red Christmas beards in the blue gulf', and consequently had no problem learning them. There were times, though, after a particularly arduous day, when I was rehearsing the scene in which Malfred had a fatal heart attack, that I wondered if that would be my lot too. For the performing dates I took a week off from teaching and although there were still plenty of other things to attend to it gave my mind a rest if nothing else. Playing the role gave me renewed strength and confidence. Ian Ralson's production was an unquestioned success and a return season was arranged for Festival Week the following January.

Patric meanwhile began creating the long-promised outdoor theatre. It was quite small – a circular space, paved in old bricks to represent the signs of the zodiac. This time there was no need to beg for help. The weather was good and a number of people volunteered – happy to lay bricks with Patric in the sunshine. One young man took annual leave and worked there every day for a week. The announcement of this new project gave Patric impish delight as it coincided with the last days of the Southern Players.

As well as evening performances of *A State of Siege* Patric decided upon a revival of *Electra,* the centre section of the *Oresteia,* to launch the open air theatre. Eve Durning played Clytaemnestra and I suspect, although Eve could never give a poor performance, that she understood the play no more than I had done. Interesting though the outdoor theatre was in itself, vision was obscured by overhanging trees and on the afternoon of the first performance a neighbour's motor-mower totally killed the show.

A State of Siege, on the other hand, had a highly satisfactory season. The city council invited us to provide a Vice-Regal Command Performance for Lord and Lady Porritt and their entourage with the appropriate social function afterwards. We gave them the choice of the two plays and they chose the New Zealand one.

For me, that was the highlight of my acting career; but how grateful I was that I had written in a brief exit from the stage early in the play. On that very special night when I thought everything would be checked and rechecked, I noticed after the first few minutes that the curtains over the windows at the back of the auditiorium had not been drawn, and in Dunedin in summer darkness does not fall until about 10 p.m. In these circumstances the blackout that marked the passage of time would have been impossible. As might be imagined my language was unprintable when I confronted the stage manager during my brief exit, and how relieved I was that he wasted no time in putting things right.

Betty Ussher had come from Timaru for Festival Week and was sufficiently impressed by the play to persuade her drama society to invite me to play Malfred Signal in a local production. Not surprisingly, audiences were fairly small at first but grew beyond our hopes during the four-night season. All my expenses were paid and I was given a small emolument. Nowadays such an enterprise would have received at least Community Arts Council support, but we were still pioneering. It is surprising though, since it has proved so successful in other countries, that amateur theatres rarely engage guest actors.

And that was not all. In those days Radio New Zealand was keen to nurture New Zealand talent. Bill Austin came to see the show and some months later invited me to redramatise the book for radio and to play Malfred Signal. Bernard Kearns was the director and his ideas for the dramatisation were very different from mine. I wondered if I had the energy – or the skill – to do it. Patric rose to the occasion. 'Ring Bernard,' he said without hesitation, 'and tell him you'll come to Christchurch and work under his guidance.'

It was good advice and I worked frenetically preparing scenes just in time to go into the studio for the recording – an exhausting but exhilarating experience. The *Listener* review of the broadcast was headed 'Perfect Listening'.

My stage version of *A State of Siege* has had two productions in Wellington by other companies and in 1980, while I was in Levin directing my comedy *I Can Give You a Bed*, I was invited to play Malfred again with Pauline Cattell's group at Avon Valley, twelve kilometres north of Levin. The president of the Manawatu Music and Drama Society saw the show and I was invited to play Malfred in Palmerston North with a good local cast. By that time I was living in Wellington but I was unable to interest anyone there.

Patric's second version of *She Stoops to Conquer* was an immaculate production with Cilla McQueen as Kate, and Eric Herd and Pamela Pow as Mr and Mrs Hardcastle. Pimple, Kate's maid, was played by Margaret Austin who wrote the sensational novels *Amsterdam Affair* and *Naked Lady* and now rejoices in the assumed title of the Duchess of Wellington.

When we did our first production of this delightful play I had taken great pride in the beautiful eighteenth-century costumes we managed to create, and started immediately collecting materials in the hope that we could do even better in the future. But Patric had been given some rolls of white map paper from which he made an effective set of simple screens with narrow black surrounds, and decided the whole production should be in black and white. No doubt thinking he was saving me trouble, he invited Betty Duncan to take charge of the costumes.

Although I was quite disappointed at first, I must say Betty did a superb job not only designing, but for the most part making, costumes of beautiful brocades and lace. This took some ingenuity for the committee gave her a float of only forty dollars.

In the anniversary booklet Pamela Pow said:

Costuming has always been a strong point in Globe productions. Many I made myself, but I can remember others; in *The Applecart* I wore a black velvet and feather creation by Els Noordhof, and in *The Sea* a floating green creation by Maureen Hitchings. Then there was my black and white costume for Patric's second production of *She Stoops to Conquer* in which the pattern of the hand-painted material concealed nudes among bunches of roses …

I doubt if any member of the audience appreciated the joke but the cast certainly did.

About this time an unexpected invitation came from the Christchurch Repertory Society inviting Patric to direct a play for them. The choice was Bernard Shaw's *You Never Can Tell*. The opportunity to concentrate on one play without having other responsibilities was just what Patric needed. The organisation was good, he liked the play and his cast, and I hoped there would be a little extra cash at the end of it.

Like many families in similar situations, the children and I enjoyed a much more relaxed approach to life when Father was away, even though we all had extra duties. Christopher and Belinda were never very keen on helping in the house. Christopher had an after-school job at the University Book Shop, and Belinda was always busy looking after a variety of animals and birds and making music. But in the theatre they were wonderfully helpful. Christopher became one of our more capable operators of sound and light, Belinda helped Patric building sets and making properties, and both were always willing to take their turn ushering, selling programmes or helping with coffee or the box office. In Patric's absence there were other responsibilities for me, including a little extra teaching at the Mosgiel seminary, though fortunately he had made other arrangements for Knox College.

A change can be as good as a rest, but we looked forward eagerly to Patric's return. Life was not complete for us without him. On the appointed day I prepared a good chicken dinner, which was ready to serve on his arrival. Over a drink before the meal he informed us he had not been happy with the billet provided by the society and had moved into a very nice motel. There he had enjoyed great comfort and a tranquil atmosphere but when he rabbited on about the wonderful food, our faces must have stated clearly what we felt. My preparations were disregarded and Patric said to the ecstatic children, 'Go and put on your best clothes, we're going to Cherry Court for dinner'.

The Christchurch production of *You Never Can Tell* was very well reviewed, but Patric felt he could do even better on his home ground with his own team of actors. Certainly, though *You Never Can Tell* is a particularly difficult play, it was a very enjoyable production. Peggy Jowett, who had not long before made a moving Antigone in a studio production of Sophocles' version, was his choice for Dolly, while Valentine was played by Michael Stedman.

Michael first came into our orbit as a young child helping his mother with properties for the Repertory Society's *Maria Marten*. He appeared in small parts at the Globe while still very young; then we lost sight of him for a while. He reappeared playing the lute for *Twelfth Night* and as a stage assistant for *The Winter's Tale* in which Peggy played a Court Lady. In *You Never Can Tell* they were cast as lovers.

By the end of the season they had become great friends and before the end of the year we attended their marriage beside the river near Outram – a truly happy occasion. Their marriage and their careers have been very successful. Having taken up a junior lectureship in geography at Victoria University in Wellington, Peggy returned to Dunedin to follow in her mother's footsteps as a potter. After putting himself through university Michael joined Dunedin television which he described as 'the logical extension of the Globe'. From there he rose to be head of training for television in Sydney and then one of the chief executives for the whole of Australia. His work took him all over the world, but he came back to Dunedin to work in the natural history section of *Wild South*, the programme that was to win sixty international awards and sell to forty different countries.

CHAPTER XIII

New Directions

Eliot – Joyce – guest productions

ë❧

One of the joys of Shakespeare's plays is that no amount of research and scholarship can lay down hard and fast rules for their production. The language is such that its music can be exciting delivered by competent actors without any trappings, as was clearly illustrated to me later by the Wellington Shakespeare Society. Nevertheless, there is scope for all kinds of interpretations, and being one of the more popular dramas, *Hamlet* has taken its share of experimentation and gimmickry. Patric had already worked on the play three times. Now he launched into an edited version he titled *Hamlet 2000*. Judicious cutting gave it an entirely new slant, making Hamlet an existentialist and Ophelia a drug addict.

Another of television's bright young directors, Ross Johnston, made a brittle, incisive Hamlet. When I met up with him recently he said:

> I even went to see flat old Strindberg. I remember *Easter* and *The Father* and plays that strike at the core of your being. Where would you see those plays today? Reading great books or being in great plays when you're very young – it sometimes takes decades to understand and appreciate them. That's the tragedy of commercial theatre. Great plays rarely get performed – in Dunedin anyway.

James Mack (later director of the Dowse Gallery in Lower Hutt, the National Museum, and in 1992, of Art at Expo in Barcelona) was lecturing at the teachers' college in Dunedin at the time. Patric invited him to design the set and costumes.

The set consisted of a steeply raked stage covered in silver building paper with black surrounds. The court characters (two of whom were played by clergymen) disported silver papier mâché breastplates, with bare midriffs and short lap-laps of black velvet edged with silver lamé. They all wore white tights and soft black shoes. Long black plastic chicken-mesh cloaks hung from the shoulders of the king and queen, which made a fascinating swooshing sound when they walked. All the royal heads were surmounted by helmets of silver papier mâché of singularly phallic design. These extraordinary outfits were completed with appropriate handmade jewellery.

Before the show, James conducted a seminar on jewellery-making for the stage. It fell to Bonny Hampton, one of our most ardent and hardworking supporters, to clean up after them. 'The dirtiest mess ever!' she declared. 'I'll never forgive him.'

He wasn't very popular either when he was making breastplates for the soldiers. One young man had a very hairy chest and James omitted to take the necessary precautions when making the plaster cast. When it came to removing the cast, well – I leave the young man's vocabulary to your imagination. Nothing, however, could detract from James's creative ability.

The final scene of *Hamlet 2000* was supported by film projections in colour – a rare departure in the early seventies – organised by Michael Stedman who greatly relished the opportunity to be so innovative. The film had to be sent to Australia for processing and we were thrown into paroxyms of anxiety by its last minute arrival, leaving no time for proper rehearsal.

If the whole idea didn't totally gel, one cannot but wonder what Patric might have achieved given a proper budget, equipment, staff, and time for preparation. I still hoped that if we left the Globe before he was totally played out that he might have such an opportunity. In the meantime he worked as conscientiously as ever.

It is not easy to stand aside, as I had found myself, but having once done so I could thoroughly enjoy being an ordinary member of the audience. Unquestionably the most memorable of guest productions that year was Ian Ralston's *Othello*. Patric was invited to play Desdemona's father, Brabantio, and of course the temptation was too great. Though he had vowed for years that he would never go on the stage except in emergencies he had become a very competent actor and admitted that he thoroughly enjoyed being on the boards.

Ian had assembled a great cast with Lyndal Howley (a former Miss New Zealand) a most attractive, vital Desdemona. John Fairmaid, who usually played sympathetic roles, was the villainous Iago with a sly sense of humour. David Baldock (currently head of Ninnox Films) as Roderigo could well have been a serious rival to Othello. Phillip Smithells and Chris Pickard, the well-known costume designer, were also in the cast.

I had some misgivings when I heard Ian was to direct and play the title role in *Othello* but when I saw the result I was delighted. Ian gave a powerful performance himself and the play moved at a lively pace. Here, I felt, was Patric's undoubted successor as director of the Globe. But Patric showed no interest in working elsewhere, vowing that when he did leave he would retire to Mahinerangi to plant trees.

Patric had a longstanding love of the work of T.S. Eliot. He read his poems and memorised many of them as soon as they were published. In the fifties he did a memorable production of *Murder in the Cathedral* in Christchurch, a sophisticated version of *The Confidential Clerk* for the Wellington Repertory Society, and at the Globe, *The Cocktail Party*, the play that caused such a stir in the West End of London in the late forties. It begins as a traditional drawing-room play but in the last act develops into a drama of disturbing intensity. Now with the exception of *The Elder Statesman*, which Mary Middleditch was to direct at the Globe later, the Eliot cycle was completed with *The Confidential Clerk*. How many directors have four Eliot plays to their credit with two produced twice?

In spite of tiredness and considerable pain from a hip, Patric was not prepared to give up until he had directed certain favourite plays, and the fact that he could not rest was a major concern. Unbeknown to him I tried various means to arrange for him to take a holiday for he was becoming increasingly difficult to live with.

One day while we were at lunch, there was a knock at the front door – obviously someone wanting costumes and without an appointment. When I rose from the table Patric said, 'Don't answer it!' I was quite happy to go, but Patric was insistent. Partly, I suppose, because I resented being dictated to, and partly for the reason I gave, I replied, 'We need the money!'

Without a word Patric rose from the table and retreated to his office in the cottage, where there happened to be an old iron bedstead. Later in the day he collected a few personal belongings and never lived in the big house again. He brought us some supplies and he and I would have quiet times together over coffee or lunch, but the pressure of trying to establish quality theatre in Dunedin had finally become too much. Now, at least, he was free from people and the telephone and could have a little peace and quiet.

Though I believed I still had something to offer I seemed to have no real place at the Globe. When I spoke to Patric of my feeling of lost identity he said, 'Why don't you get something of your own to do, quite apart from the theatre?'

Shortly afterwards I was invited to become a charter member of Zonta, a service club for women who were leaders in their own field, and who raised funds for a variety of worthy causes. It involved considerable expense and time but after some deliberation I accepted.

During a visit to Wellington I saw Molly Cook and Alice Gray demonstrating their fabulous period costumes and jewellery, and learnt that they would present this fascinating show for any just cause. They were happy to come all the way to Dunedin at their own expense since Molly wished to visit her aunt Miss Theomin, the last member of the family to live at Olveston, the stately home that has since become such a popular tourist attraction.

I undertook to arrange programmes for both Zonta and the Globe. Zonta organised their evening with their usual efficiency but it was an uphill task interesting a new committee of the Friends and I was left to do most of the work, including begging people to come. What an opportunity was lost! Times like this justified Patric's reticence to work with committees.

Shortly after this I suggested to the Friends that they might like to entertain English author J.B. Priestley who, I discovered, was visiting New Zealand. They liked the idea and arranged a function that was so well attended there was barely standing room. The august gentleman arrived very late, by which time the Globe function was in full swing. In the book he wrote on his return home, Priestley wrote:

> Having accepted the engagement I did what I imagine most people do, I treated myself to a picture of what would happen. I saw myself meeting a small group of enthusiasts and then asking or answering questions, giving them, if they wanted it, the benefit of my years of theatrical experience, which was extensive and not limited to the writing of plays. And I was quite wrong.

> Nothing of the sort had been planned. True, I was shown – and asked to admire – the stage and the tiny 80-seat auditorium that had been ingeniously contrived out of what had been part of a private house. But instead of a serious small group, wanting to ask and to answer equally serious questions, what I found was a large noisy party, apparently consisting of people no more interested in me and the present and future of the Theatre than I was in the statistics of the timber trade ... I didn't see why I should have been put under pressure then compelled to forsake an agreeable dinner party, just to catch this babble of self-important performers and a few superior patrons of this minikin experimental Theatre.

I still had a great number of classes and private pupils at the Globe, and was also asked to return to St Hilda's for three classes a week. I found this exhausting but illuminating. The unruliness I used to expect in the fourth form was now apparent in Form 1, and the overall standard of speech and manners had been what I suppose I must call 'liberalised'. I would not like to be a full-time classroom teacher today.

On the plus side educationalists were becoming aware of the value of drama in schools and I was invited to give a paper at the Primary Teachers' Association (PTA) conference which was held in Dunedin that year. The topic was 'Creative Drama in the Classroom'. The lecture-demonstration was held at the Globe for which I was truly grateful as I had a severe dose of flu. I looked forward to attending other sessions but when I went to bed that night I fell into a deep sleep and did not stir till half-past four the following day.

Patric and Belinda were at the lake; Christopher had a holiday job at the University Book Shop, so I saw little of him. Towards the end of the week when I was still in bed he told me John Griffin had offered him a full-time job. It was only a few weeks before his University Entrance examination. He hated school but promised he would continue his studies, and I felt he had excellent prospects with John as his guide and mentor. I was feeling so ill I wondered how long I would be able to continue working and Patric's future was uncertain to say the least. Christopher accepted the offer, and it was many years before he went inside an educational institute again.

Patric embarked upon 1972 refreshed after and a good holiday at the lake and several weeks in Gore directing *Who's Afraid of Virginia Woolf?* In conjunction with the Friends he devised an ambitious but exciting programme for the next two years after which he vowed he would retire, replacement director or no.

Directors were arranged for the four guest productions, and it was announced that 'from now on the Globe will aim to expand the activities of the theatre on a regional basis' and that it would become a Community Arts Centre.

On the strength of this we brought the Gore production of *Who's Afraid of Virginia Woolf?* to the Globe in Festival Week. It was a good production but Gore people are very hospitable and having come such a long way inevitably expected something like the splendid parties they had given us in the past. I had deliberately left arrangements to the Friends but nothing seemed to be happening. I rushed to our meagrely stocked kitchen – we had no deep-freeze and only very small cupboards – and in record time produced a pile of the bean fritters which had become almost legendary at the Globe.

In the holidays I directed a play for the university students for their brief schools tour. My choice was Bernard Shaw's *A Man of Destiny*, a pleasant little play about Napoleon when he was a very young army general. I love working with young people so this was a happy time for me.

In most situations it was I who followed in Patric's wake but now he decided to direct Shakespeare's *Much Ado About Nothing*, which I had done at St Hilda's College in 1958. It had all the elements of a happy production with Cilla McQueen and attractive newcomer Nick Round-Turner in the leads.

With the Friends now more firmly in control it was decided that *Much Ado* should be staged in the Mayfair Theatre in South Dunedin with a view to attracting school parties and bigger audiences. The Mayfair is a fine old theatre, which the Dunedin Opera Company (inspired by our building efforts) had restored for their own use. It was ideal for them but a little large for a straight play, especially in an unusual locality, for most of our regular clientele. Why it wasn't first played at the Globe I shall never know. Our audiences would have loved it. The Empire-line costumes were delightful and the set boasted a fountain that actually worked, thanks to the ingenuity of Graeme Smith. Bookings, however, were a disaster. It transpired that the committee member responsible for publicity had gone out of town and no one else had done anything!

It was not long before another of the grand ideas fell apart. The proposed director of James Joyce's *Exiles* withdrew. I was surprised that it had been given to an inexperienced director in the first place. It is a complex play and a favourite of Patric's, so it was inevitable that he should take over the production himself.

He assembled a great team – Marilyn Parker, Ian Ralston, Terry MacTavish, Murray Hutchinson, Betty Hudson and twelve-year-old Mark Williamson. With this group, all of whom were familiar with his method of working, Patric was at last able to put into practice a policy he had been working towards for some time. He outlined the set – a room with windows down one side into which we looked through a cutaway wall with a pathway around it. Patric placed four chairs outside the acting area, and told the cast to put them in position if and where

Above: Belinda Carey as the maid in Penny For a Song, *by Whiting 1972.*
Below: Saint's Day, *by Whiting. A difficult play to design, Patric sought the help of Betty Duncan, whose painting is suspended between the two tiers, 1972.*

Above: Rodney Kennedy in 1975. (Photograph by Gary Blackman.)
Below: Rosalie Carey's Edendale Station, 1981. Left to right: Michele Amas, Bill Daker, Louise Green and Tony Bamford. (Critic)

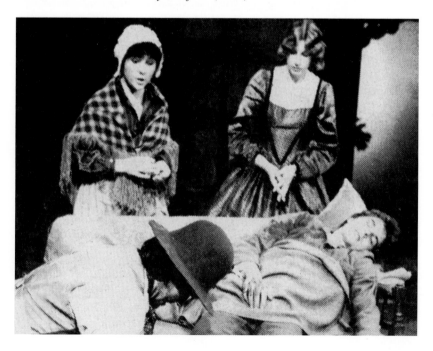

they felt the need. Moves were left almost entirely to the discretion of the actors, provided of course that they were consistent once plotting had settled down. (I have seen the idea tried in a less suitable situation with far from satisfactory results but this team enjoyed the challenge, and it worked.)

During rehearsals young Mark Williamson broke an arm – but having an arm in plaster maybe added a touch of realism. Then Ian Ralston sprained an ankle. That was a different matter and meant the first night had to be postponed. In spite of these misfortunes *Exiles* was a beautiful, sensitive production – one of Patric's best.

A delegation from the Arts Council came to see it. Sunny Amey, erstwhile director of the National Drama School, who was one of their number, expressed her envy that Patric should have the opportunity to direct such a wonderful but difficult play. Patric's reply was that the Globe was available to anyone who wished to direct a quality play provided they could cope with the conditions under which we worked.

The other members of the delegation were noticeably silent but they did manage to give us a grant of $2,000. Naturally we were pleased with this but at the same time Downstage Theatre in Wellington was given $40,000 and the Auckland Theatre Trust no less than $80,000. Being so isolated and so busy it was hard to keep in touch with what went on in other centres, but much later we learned that community theatres began by paying their actors four dollars a week – so they were obviously only part-time professionals.

Fortunately there were competent directors in Dunedin foolish enough to work under Globe conditions during the next few months. James Mack had already written and directed a rather risqué revue entitled *A Hole Whirled in a Cup of Mince* for which he organised set and costumes as well.

John Dawson, lecturer in the German department of the university and later its head, directed *Dance Boy for Rain* written by Dunedin poet Alan Loney, who described the play as 'an act in five plays … each sketch is a sort of stage in a central character's life'.

John also translated and directed *Ring-a-Ring-a-Rosie*, a charming little play by German playwright Schnitzler and on a visit to the Globe in later years I saw him give a remarkable performance in an up-to-date translation of Molière's *La Malade Imaginaire*. As well as his undoubted talent in the theatre, John was a singularly active president of the Friends of the Globe for many years and worked extremely hard in that capacity.

And there were productions by Alan Curreri (now a professional actor in the United States), Louise Petherbridge (who had recently returned from working in the English professional theatre), and Rowena Cullen (who became the driving force at the Globe for many years).

John Bailey came to Dunedin from Auckland especially to work in the type of play we did at the Globe. Huntly Elliott (professional actor, producer of radio drama, and television director) procured the professional rights, and gave us a sophisticated production of Christopher Hampton's *The Philanthropist*, which had enjoyed singular success in the West End; and Terry Bryan, also from television staff, directed James Saunders' *Next Time I'll Sing to You*.

This wealth of enthusiasm and talent suggested that the Globe could manage well enough without the Careys.

For my own part I was becoming quite crafty in devising ways and means of conserving energy. Rather than undertake a separate production at St Hilda's I hit upon John Dunmore's *Appendix to Captain Cook's Voyage* which illustrates in a delightful manner our inability to understand the customs of other peoples. The play was staged at the Globe using our actors for the main parts, with all my senior girls as Tahitian maidens. Of course there were hurdles to overcome. Contrary to the original arrangement reorganisation of the programme meant that my rehearsal time fell on either side of the school holidays. It also meant that the new dates took us right into winter, by which time the dusky maidens had lost their summer tan and I couldn't afford enough lotion to rectify the situation. They looked less like Tahitians than nymphs from Mars.

My final contribution to the main programme was *The Horse*, wonderfully clever satire by Julius Hay which comments on the egocentricities of dictators and, as I told the *Otago Daily Times*:

> It highlights the incredible fashion-following to which young people are so vulnerable, and secondly the respect we have for horses. I noticed recently that a longer obituary was given to a racehorse than to one of our more important artists.

Undoubtedly the most ambitious guest production of 1972 was Ian Ralston's *Richard II* (Shakespeare). As in *Othello* Ian not only directed but also took part himself, this time as the political realist Bolingbroke, while the idealist Richard, who ruled by divine right, was in the skilled hands of Huntly Elliott. Lyndal Howley made a sensitive and attractive Queen, with Huntly's wife, Shirley, as the Queen Mother. Once again

Patric could not resist taking a part and Christopher, along with a number of my teenage students, was also in the cast.

Because of the numbers involved Ian decided to stage the play in Allen Hall, where he had an extensive apron stage erected with virtually no other scenery. Once again Ian amazed us with his ability to direct and act. Because of severe back problems at the time I dreaded sitting on a hard seat during a long play, but it was more than worth it and, though some of the small-part actors were very young and inexperienced, the overall effect was most impressive. Ian and Huntly Elliott worked well together and could have held their own in any professional company.

Regrettably, in spite of excellent press notices, apart from schools, Dunedin audiences were a bitter disappointment. Ian lashed out through the *Otago Daily Times*:

> In five days no more than one hundred and twenty adults have so far been to see Shakespeare's *Richard II* ... As far as I'm concerned that's it. Before I do another major outside production of Shakespeare, the theatrical climate will need to be considerably changed.

Whether wisely or not he had the courage to dismiss as 'cultural slobs and lip-servers the so-called theatre-going public of Dunedin ...'

But *Richard II* was not dead and went on to play in Gore and Invercargill later in September. The Gore visit went smoothly but in Invercargill the drama was not confined to the stage. The car Christopher was driving (we did not have one of our own) was involved in a motor accident. Trying to find the way to their billet after setting up the stage, he avoided a fast moving car but hit a power pole. Christopher and his three young companions were taken off to hospital. When he caught up with what had happened, Ian watched the clock with trepidation and finally went in search of his cast. Quite apart from shock, all four had minor injuries and the doctor in charge was in no hurry to release them.

'Can they walk'? Ian demanded. They could, and he laughed when he recalled telling the duty doctor that he was happy to bring his young charges back later, 'but right now the show must go on!' The performance was delayed for half an hour but as might be expected the adrenalin ran high and all went well. Ian recalls one moment when Huntly very nearly lost his cool. Just as he delivered a line about it being a time to bleed, he looked at Christopher. Blood was beginning to seep through the bandage on his head. The line was just too near the bone, as you might say.

Since our departure, the Globe has done a Shakespearean production almost every year. My one regret is that they have not restored the theatre to its original state with the tarras and casement windows with doors beneath, or better still a simple two-tiered stage resembling the reconstructed Globe in London, but this could happen in the future.

CHAPTER XIV

Winding Down

The Globe's Legacy to the City

෨

Many theatrical producers and directors are reputed to have affairs with their actors – male or female. Patric claimed he had one with each of his leading ladies – but it was always essentially intellectual. He also enjoyed affairs of a different nature – a passionate involvement with whatever dramatist he was working with at any given time. For instance, we were all aware of his love-hate relationship with Shakespeare as well as his longstanding affection for T.S. Eliot. Then there was an era when Tennessee Williams was his passion but, in his last years at the Globe, Patric was to embark on an infatuation with English dramatist John Whiting.

He considered Whiting to be the greatest English dramatist since John Webster – whom he rated above Shakespeare. We were still in England when the young playwright won the Festival of Britain Arts Theatre prize. He was rubbished by the critics – I can remember some of their fatuous comments such as suggesting it may be necessary to stand on one's head in the aisle in order to understand the play. In London, *Saint's Day* ran for only three weeks and it was ten years before it was revived.

'It must be conceded that Whiting is a complex writer,' Patric told the *Otago Daily Times:*

> *Saint's Day* embodies its sophisticated ideas in a forceful and realistic dramatic framework, evoked with economy and skill, and a surprising beauty of language. This realistic framework heightens the importance of the ideas and questions Whiting raises in the play – questions such as the relationship of the artist to society, and the endless question of violence in man ...

Patric set about studying the corpus of Whiting's work, and planned to direct at least three of the plays. Only the finest of our actors could play the difficult roles and Whiting had limited audience appeal; but in view of the complexity of the writing of Eliot and Whiting, patrons were invited to come to the theatre on the first Sunday of each season for talks and discussions about the plays, with Patric and the casts, followed by the usual tea and biscuits.

Fortunately in each case Patric assembled a splendid team with such talented people as Cilla McQueen, Ian Ralston, Bill Mackay, Stephen McElrea, and Terry MacTavish (daughter of Shona Dunlop who has contributed so much to the dance scene and written two excellent books). Whiting also made considerable demands on the designer. Patric's normal routine after a first night was to have a quiet day – going to town or tending his roses – but by the next day he was ready to launch into building the set for the forthcoming production. When it came to *Saint's Day*, he admitted quietly over a cup of coffee, 'This set has beaten me; for the first time in my life, I don't know where to begin!'

How well I understood the feeling of having dragged every idea from oneself till one felt like 'the pelican in her piety' with no one but oneself to turn to.

Saint's Day required a two-tiered set with a huge painting suspended between the two floors. Betty Duncan, now an authority on Pacific religious studies, was at this time developing her skill as a visual artist and had done some exciting paintings of the plays. (The one she did of *The Cocktail Party* has pride of place in my home.) She had already been asked to paint the big picture required for *Saint's Day* and now Patric sought her help with the set itself. Between them the problems were solved, and from then on Betty's youth, intelligence, and imagination became very important to Patric.

Saint's Day was followed by *Marching Song* in which Patric played, appropriately, the role of an ageing artist. The third Whiting play (which was actually first performed in 1948) was very different. *A Penny for a Song* was written in a happy period in Whiting's life and is appropriately lighthearted; but beneath the hilarity the play shows the absurdity of armed conflict, and Whiting's deep concern with the problem of responsibility for war and its resultant suffering.

Happy though this production was, it had an unfortunate consequence for one of our most valued members. The play is set in the Napoleonic era, and requires a steam engine and a canon on the stage – and marvellous creations they were, largely evolved by Belinda. An over-loud blast from the canon caused Walter Bloomfield to go deaf in one ear – a serious handicap for a teacher of German and French in a secondary school.

The final and greatest of the Whiting plays, *The Devils*, was to be Patric's swansong. There was a superb Gothic set by Ralph Hotere; Rodney Kennedy looked after the costumes; and the cast of almost thirty included Huntly Elliott, Cilla McQueen, Terry MacTavish, John Bailey, Murray Hutchinson, David and Peter Baldock and, undeterred by his previous experience, Walter Bloomfield.

My personal recollection of the play was one of overwhelming power with unforgettable performances by Huntly Elliott and Cilla McQueen. The moment when Huntly (Grandier) prostrated himself on the stage with arms outstretched is one I shall never forget. I could find no newspaper write-ups, and recently Cilla recollected:

> It was the most difficult part I have ever played, but the most rewarding – extraordinary language. Plays like that have had an enormous effect on my writing, because although I majored in English at university, I would never have encountered the plays and the in-depth discussions with Patric. Learning roles by heart helped to stock up the language bank, vocabulary and imagery.

Apart from the scene mentioned, Huntly told me that he too remembered little about the play itself, but he does recall

> … sitting on the foyer stairs after performances winding down, glass in hand, talking with Patric and other members of the cast, about the play, theatre in general and everything else.

The final performance, on 24 November 1973 was followed by a champagne supper as a farewell to Patric (seat and supper $5). It was an emotional occasion. Patric was presented with a tree and a wheelbarrow. According to Huntly, Patric's comment was that he has always had an ambition to sit under a tree and watch a wheelbarrow.

Not long before, an 'Important Globe Meeting' had been announced in the press for the purpose of electing a new committee, and discussing the possible sale of all or part of 102 London Street (the property next door to the theatre with the Victorian cottage on it) as well as 'the possible closing of the theatre, resiting or building a new one, and the possibility of becoming professional or semi-professional'.

As in many similar statements made by the Friends or by Patric himself, it was suggested that after leaving the Globe, Patric would continue to freelance in the theatre and return for guest productions, but in the meantime he could look no further than retiring to Mahinerangi.

The newsletter that announced *The Devils* and Patric's retirement also stated that many of the Globe's problems had been resolved: 'On a more basic level, the toilets are progressing steadily, an impressive amount of clay having been shifted. Much loving labour has also gone into the garden …'

More importantly, whereas an advertisement for an artistic director the previous year had drawn a complete blank, resulting in our staying on for another year, it was now announced that the responsibility was being taken over by another individualist of impressive talent – Rodney Kennedy. After a quiet spell following his retirement as drama specialist for University Extension he was bursting with fresh ideas that promised an interesting year's activity in 1974.

This was a great relief to us all, especially for me since I had already taken the plunge and accepted the offer of a very cheap fare to England in a six-berth cabin with the Dawson family. I had little idea what I would use for money, but I took a boarder and was working and saving hard. I needed a change and had a very real obligation to fulfil with my aunt in Cornwall who was ageing quickly and seemed determined that I should come, suggesting that she might not still be alive if I waited another year.

I applied to the Arts Council for a travel grant and duly went to Wellington for an interview – a nerve-wracking experience saved only by Sunny Amey's humanity. While in Wellington I was advised to apply for funds from the British Council as well, which of course I did. By chance I met up with Alex Fry, who was then literary editor of the *Listener.*

He was naturally interested in Patric's future and suggested an article might be appropriate. I welcomed the idea because I was sure that, like Rodney, there would soon come a time when Patric would want to work again and it would help if it were known that he was available. The article, from which I quoted earlier, took the form of an interview with O.E. Middleton, a former Burns Fellow who had decided, like many other artists, to continue to live in Dunedin after his tenure of office had expired.

Patric told him:

> The point about the Globe Theatre is that it always made a profit in terms of what we spent on such things as the set and advertising. A small profit of about say $20 a year was eaten up on the $12,000 we spent on building the theatre. I don't know how it was built or how it was paid for; but it has been paid for.

That gave us considerable pride. Whereas so many enterprises have left business and tradespeople out of pocket, we were able to leave Dunedin not owing anyone a cent.

The *Listener* article continued:

[P.C.] What have we done? 178 plays in 12 years. The danger here is that of course you can't do 178 plays in 12 years and do them well.

[O.E.M.] No, that's true. But I think your achievement, Patric, has been that the peaks have been very high indeed.

I believe Patric was pleased that he was not entirely forgotten by the outside world, but over all the interview reflected a man who was tired, and somewhat disillusioned, and would have little enthusiasm for work in another theatre.

After the farewell party for *The Devils* Patric slipped away as soon as was decently possible. He had arranged for Christopher to take him to the Lake that very night, saying that if he didn't go while he was still on a high he wondered if he would ever go at all. He had given so much of himself, he was completely burnt out. How thankful I was that we had the Mahinerangi property for him to flee to. I believe he would have maintained a happy relationship with the Globe, but a conscientious treasurer paid him only till the end of November, rather than for the whole of the financial year. In most situations such things can be sorted out but, given Patric's vulnerable condition, not even to be allowed normal holiday pay meant that his disillusionment knew no bounds.

Apart from the day he and some friends collected my piano, which Sadie Foote had sold to me at 'mates rates' because it could not be tuned to concert pitch, he has never set foot inside a theatre again.

David Greet of the commercial television staff, who became chairman of the Friends committee shortly after we left, said of him in the anniversary booklet:

Patric was a dynamo. When he got it into his head to produce a play, usually some obscure work by some equally obscure playwright, nothing would stop his enthusiasm ... He had the uncanny ability of getting people motivated and to get the best out of people off the street and turn them into actors overnight ... *The Cocktail Party* was the first Globe production I had been involved in and was quite an eye-opener for me.

Patric lived and worked theatre. It was his life blood, he produced, directed, choreographed, made sets, designed costumes, if necessary acted ... he was the whole production, he lived it all from start to finish. Patric was the Globe and it very nearly became his epitaph when he retired. Such was his following that it was only the stubbornness of a small group who refused to see a good thing die that enabled the Theatre to carry on against overwhelming odds of sentimentality. The ghost of Patric however lingered on for a long time.

He was a great teacher, an inspired director, and a stimulating conversationalist who loved all the good things of life – essentially a man of champagne tastes on a beer income.

And what had we achieved in all this time? Materially, virtually nothing. But we had, to say the least, taken a conservative Victorian city, or part of it, into the twentieth century in terms of the arts. I say part of it because I recall going to a mayoral reception in 1963 to herald the opening of a Spring Arts Festival. Our offering was a double bill of avant garde theatre. In his address the mayor warned, 'You may not like some of the modern work presented but we must remember we are in a new century.'

When we left the Globe the people of Dunedin had seen the work of some of the country's best known visual artists – Colin McCahon, Ralph Hotere, Donald McAra, Michael Illingworth, Tom Esplin, Para Matchitt, Jeffrey Harris, Els Noordhof, John Brown, Marilynn Webb, John Coley, Bill Mackay; potters Beryl Jowett, Len Castle, Doreen Blumhardt, Barry Brickell; sculptors John Middleditch and Tanya Ashken – as well as some who were new.

Patric had commissioned Nigel Eastgate, Peter Platt, Anthony Elton, John Wesley Barker, and Anthony Watson to compose music for his productions, and Christopher Norton had provided new music for two of mine. We had produced a host of new plays and broadened the experience of innumerable young people who have since risen to the top of their professions.

By closely collaborating with the university music department, Patric had kept us in touch with the most up-to-date – as well as classical – music, playing and discussing it during set and theatre building as well as using it for the plays.

We had dance programmes and poetry readings – one with as many as thirteen recognised poets on the stage at one time, another featuring the Liverpool Beat Poets with the readers all dressed in handprinted garments made by two of our members whose work we wanted to promote. There were jazz and classical concerts, coffee mornings with guest speakers, and lecture-demonstrations – such as when Ken Smith introduced us to the art of trumpet playing. There were weekend seminars – and others that extended over a number of weeks – for actors, playwrights, and fencers. We hosted the seminar for visiting English playwright, David Campton, entertained Trinity College and New Zealand Speech Board examiners, visiting university lecturers and artists such as Larry Adler, William Clausen, Inia Te Wiata, and Catherine de Segne with the Treteau de Paris Company. There was a fancy-dress ball, pre-show dinners, and innumerable after-show parties.

Roger Hall and Renée workshopped plays at the Globe; in our day, as well as the nine plays by James K. Baxter there was my dramatisation of the Janet Frame novel and new plays by Warren Dibble, Peter Olds, Alex Guyan, and Michael Noonan. After we left, John Caselberg, R.A.K. Mason, James McNeish, Bill Sewell, Ivan Daichie, Dick Boraman, Iain Lonie, Frank Grayson, Simon O'Connor, Hone Tuwhare, and Michael-Anne Forster joined the list.

In a recent letter to me, Michael-Anne Forster wrote:

> I also acted in my own plays under the capable direction of Jenny Wake, who eventually went on to form her own Children's Theatre Company in Wellington. (Calico Theatre Co). The Globe gave me confidence, experience and a wonderful set of friends, who like me, were dedicated to the art of 'pretend'.

With the help of our loyal supporters, 'the graveyard of theatre' had become the birthplace of an incredible upsurge of artistic expression. Sir William and Lady Rosemary Southgate maintained that we had advanced the arts in New Zealand by at least twenty years.

The city had bought the fine old Regent Theatre for live shows; the Dunedin Opera Company was flourishing in South Dunedin at the Mayfair Theatre, and had launched several international careers.

The Repertory Society had its own home at the Playhouse and was in good heart, largely due to the tireless efforts of Ruby and Jack Hannan. There was a flourishing drama department at the university and we had developed a fine core of actors who were ready to establish a professional company.

Plans were afoot for making the Globe a public theatre and so be eligible to become at least partly professional. Before this was in place, though, Huntly Elliott, Murray Hutchinson and Alex Gilchrist, along with David Carnegie of the university drama department, had set the wheels in motion and by July 1974 the Fortune Theatre was launched in the tiny Cine-Club in which we had enjoyed such success with our productions of *Oedipus* and *Antigone* all those years before.

CHAPTER XV

Rock Bottom

England and Wellington

❧

Patric's departure did not mean that I could relax. Belinda was still at school and I had my term's teaching to complete. Whether I would go to England was now in doubt, for though I had scraped up the one-way fare I had insufficient to bring myself back, and was relying on extra work, little of which eventuated. However my good mother offered to help if I would return via America and visit my brother in California. So it was confirmed that I should make the trip.

After many abortive plans, arrangements were finally made for a young couple with a two-year-old child to share the house with Belinda and a cousin. The promising thing was that the wife was a speech teacher so I handed over all my teaching materials and my pupils to her. I fled to Mahinerangi, looking forward to a little while with my family before leaving for England. Typically, one of our members who would have been alone for the festive season arrived to spend it with us.

Enthused by having been to a Theatre Federation acting course, Christopher had applied to go to drama school in Wellington; Patric had been asked by sympathisers on the Arts Council if he would accept a $6,000 bursary, and I of course awaited the results of my two applications for travel grants.

On Christmas Eve 1973 the neighbours brought our mail. There were four important letters. A change of government and the consequent reshuffle of personnel meant that there was no fellowship for Patric; Christopher had not been accepted for drama school; but for me, the Queen Elizabeth II Arts Council offered $500 'to carry out the programme of studies submitted', and the British Council £150 'towards the cost of travel and subsistence in connection with professional visits'.

I would have preferred either one of the other two to have benefited. All I wanted was a rest. I had great hopes that the sea voyage would put me right, but the ship was overcrowded and very noisy, and each time I went ashore I spent the next day prostrate in my bunk.

The British Council had booked accommodation for my first four days in London after which David Mitchell (now Warbeck) gave me a bed. Mercifully, Peter Tulloch was also there on an Arts Council bursary. I was deeply distressed that I had heard nothing from my family during the voyage and more than grateful when Peter tracked Belinda down on the telephone. I realised she had been too upset at my departure to write to me.

The cousin had gone to board elsewhere, and the young couple departed after one week leaving fourteen-year-old Belinda in that big house with no locks on the doors. Bill Dacker and Alan Curreri, who were living in the cottage next door and working for the theatre, had been very supportive but neither Patric nor the Friends appeared to have taken any responsibility. Christopher was flatting and had booked to go to Australia, but before leaving he found a young couple who met with the Friends' approval to share the house with Belinda, and I was assured I need not worry further.

The British Council had arranged an interesting programme which included a weekend seminar on present day costume and a visit to the Bristol Old Vic, where David Phethean gave me a royal reception. I also saw some small underfunded theatres – the last thing I could be genuinely interested in, especially since I heard endless moans about lack of support from the British Arts Council. There was, however, an unscheduled weekend at Dartington Hall where I saw a festival of experimental theatre and heard an exciting concert by The Fires of London quartet.

Then out of the blue my tall dark and handsome admirer from the past arrived in England. He too was still married but he wafted me off to Malta for the most restful and enjoyable holiday I have ever had.

Nonetheless, when I finally reached St Ives I was in a complete state of collapse. Instead of being a shining light for my eighty-three-year-old aunt, I retired to bed and she looked after me.

Since I was enjoying the benison of public money I felt I must do something in return. Back in London I arranged a programme of poetry and music with scenes from Baxter's plays, with expatriate New Zealanders. Held in the penthouse of New Zealand House – and the first of its kind – it was well publicised and attended by the High Commissioner and various other dignitaries. I enjoyed meeting up with people I had not seen for years.

Having done that, I returned to St Ives to spend time with Aunt

Helen and think about her future as well as my own. Health was a major problem and nothing came to mind that seemed to make any sense. How was I to support myself and Belinda especially since my job at St Hilda's no longer existed? The only option appeared to be the hope of an office job in Dunedin and spending weekends at Mahinerangi. To do this I needed a car. I took driving lessons but the nervous strain was too much, especially since on my first day out I narrowly missed being hit by another car.

Time went by while I strove to get myself well enough to go home. Then I decided if I were going to the States I would take the opportunity of attending the Zonta International Conference in Boston. The Dunedin branch arranged for me to be their first representative overseas. Both they and headquarters gave me financial as well as moral support. It was all rather bewildering but a wonderful experience and an insight into the capabilities of women of many nations.

On Belinda's recommendation I stopped off at Sydney where Christopher had been working for some months but was far from happy. It was agreed that he should come home. I also visited my parents in Auckland and spent a few days in Wellington to make enquiries about studying music through the Correspondence School or at the Polytechnic on Belinda's behalf, for she had walked out of school on her fifteenth birthday and had gone to live with Patric at the lake. I also enquired about jobs for myself. I assumed there would be some work for me with radio drama, and Nola Millar had earlier invited me to be the voice teacher for her drama school. This seemed a good option, but alas in the meantime Nola had died.

When I finally arrived in Dunedin, Marian Coxhead was at Air New Zealand's city depot to escort me to 104 London Street, mindful of what had happened in my absence and fearing, as was true, that I had not been informed.

The cottage at No. 102 had been sold. All the costumes that I had spent weeks carrying from the theatre and the house were on racks in my bedroom. My personal belongings were still there, some scattered on the floor, the blankets still on my bed ready for my return. The hallway and 'little studio' were stacked with props and furniture. Belinda still had her own room and as it was Saturday she was in town to attend her music lesson at the polytechnic. Instead of coming back to my elegant home and looking after my daughter, at least until she had sat School Certificate, I was virtually 'on the street'. As had been suspected, I had no wish to stay at the Globe under the circumstances and was grateful to accept Sadie Foote's offer of a divan in her dining room.

I enquired at Dunedin television and radio about work and was offered one hour a day for one week typing for Geoff Robinson in the news room at 4ZB. I took it without realising that the commercial station was almost inaccessible without a car. But I did it and it stood me in good stead later. To my surprise Belinda was accepted for music school without any suggestion that she should sit School Certificate first, and I decided there was only one course for me to take. I must go to Wellington and support her for at least the next two years.

By the time I began the job search in Wellington in 1975, the oil scare and the sinking-lid policy meant that jobs were very scarce, so after one or two abortive applications I went to Radio New Zealand. I was told there was nothing unless I was a copy typist prepared to work at odd hours in the newsroom. I had learnt touch typing and though I was not very smart on a keyboard I said, 'Okay. I'm a copy typist, and yes, I have worked in the newsroom in Dunedin.' I was asked to make a commitment for one year but I stayed for five.

After two weeks struggling with an electric typewriter, which was new to me, and the hectic but interesting programme of the newsroom, I was transferred to the typing pool and then to Broadcasts to Schools, where I spent most of the day copying radio plays. Part of the attraction of living in Wellington was the prospect of acting in radio drama. It was not usual for clerical staff to do this, but I had done some good work in Dunedin and Christchurch and the Director General seemed to know my capabilities. He gave me special dispensation to do up to fifteen hours a week in the drama studio. I applied to one of the producers with whom I had worked in the past and was told, 'Oh, but we have to keep the work for the professionals.'

I said nothing more about it until I had left broadcasting, when I suffered a further humiliation from a young man whom I had taught and given his first major part in a play. After that I settled for small parts in film and television which I greatly enjoyed and which was sometimes very remunerative.

After having been something of 'a big frog' for about twenty years I had to face the fact that I was now very small fry even in the typing pool. Determined not to accept this status without a fight, I decided I would do something to support the Bill Toft Memorial Fund, designed to improve broadcasting standards. (Bill Toft was a highly respected announcer who died at an early age.) To this end I hired the Library

Hall and invited a group of well-known broadcasters, whom I had met at various times, to read their favourite poems. They were John Gordon, Graeme Thomson, Beverley Wakem, Pauline Ritchie, Relda Familton, and Philip Sherry. At the last minute Philip Sherry had to go on duty so I joined this illustrious group myself.

My job at Broadcasts to Schools improved as time went on. I wrote some stories which were accepted for broadcast, and spent some time in the studio. However, my health continued to deteriorate. The medical profession could find no solution and I decided to try a change of work and environment.

Fortuitously in 1980, I was invited to direct a play (that developed into two) in Waipukurau, and later to direct my own comedy *I Can Give You a Bed* in Levin (opening 11 November). It had come second in a national competition and at the end of the year I was asked to conduct a drama seminar as a forerunner to a production of the play at the Globe for Festival Week (1981). Freelancing certainly agreed with me better than sitting in a office all day and this was a chance to go back and lay the ghosts in Dunedin.

The Community Arts Council offered help with my accommodation; and of course there were royalties for the play. I went South before Christmas and held auditions. It was apparent that casting the demanding leading male role was not possible, so we settled for a less difficult play of mine, *Edendale Station*, a drama set in the North Canterbury high country in 1866-67 covering the time of the great snow which is so clearly documented in Lady Barker's diaries.

The weekend seminar attracted a number of talented young people. A special feature was a champagne breakfast organised by David Manley, whose catering prowess had become quite a feature at the Globe. The participants were asked to wait in the foyer until summoned. When they were finally admitted to the theatre, they found nothing but trestle tables covered with white paper and no food. David and I handed round imaginary plates, opened bottles and poured drinks all in mime. After initial bewilderment and obvious disappointment everyone joined in what was an entertaining improvisation exercise. David appeared on cue with chicken, fresh rolls, and champagne.

By this time being at the Globe had no pain for me. Patric once said he would go to Timbuctoo to produce the plays he wanted to do, and now I was feeling the same. The Friends committee, many of them stalwarts from our era, was in good heart. The disintegrating tiled roof had been replaced. Thanks to a generous grant from the McMillan Trust and assistance from the city council a toilet block had been built onto what had been our breakfast room. The old kitchen was renovated and I heard good reports about what had taken place under the artistic directorship of Rodney Kennedy and Mary Middleditch.

Frank Grayson was living happily in the house, where he had a bedsitting room, bathroom and tiny kitchenette – originally the butler's pantry. Frank looked after us all. For *Edendale Station* he created an elegant set from flats discarded by the television studios, with interesting effects of a snowy landscape for the last act, and chunks of snow falling from the eaves at appropriate moments. Charmian Smith was my wardrobe mistress. Beautiful period costumes with delightful attention to detail – suitable socks, the handkerchief in the pocket – appeared as if by magic.

I was extremely happy with my cast. Among them we had Michelle Amas, a particularly talented actress who has since turned professional. Also in the cast were Bill Dacker, a great worker for the Globe; Ben Elson, who was in our very first independent production; and Mickie Reid, who, with her son John and daughter Beverley, has worked in a variety of capacities at the Globe and in other Dunedin theatres.

Every night old friends were in the audience, and on one occasion Brian McNeill – actor and playwright, whom I had not met before – waited till all others had left. He introduced himself and said, 'I owe you an apology. I told someone I was going to see the Mills and Boon play at the Globe, but I've thoroughly enjoyed it'.

It was a happy production, and audiences enjoyed a reflection of New Zealand social history and a play without violence or four-letter words. Suffice to say that the Globe box office returns were the best for two years.

Professionally I felt I was on the way back, but to my intense sadness my marriage to Patric seemed irretrievable and my health was a major worry. After my desperate nagging of the medical profession, it was revealed that I had serious deterioration of the liver as a result of continued stress – but I was offered no help whatsoever. Had it not been that I had written a little book on speech, which I felt must be published, I suspect I may have faded away altogether. I used what little energy I had getting it launched and one day, when I was forced to go into the city on its behalf, I met Walter Bloomfield who was working in Wellington. He saw at once that I needed help, and arranged for me to go to an excellent naturopath. I was put on a cruelly rigid diet, which I obeyed implicitly and from then on I began, very slowly, to improve.

A major setback occurred when, in August 1982, Patric announced that he wanted the marriage dissolved. He had found a cheap house and was going to live in Gore – where I suspected he had lost his heart many years before.

He left Mahinerangi in September, taking what he needed for his future quiet life, but I had further engagements planned and could not go south again until December. By the time I reached Mahinerangi, the place looked derelict. In the absence of humans, possums, rats, mice, moths and maggots had moved in. Mercifully a buyer appeared on the horizon and after much soul-searching my dream property was sold. Christopher and Belinda were both overseas. Belinda was philosophical but Christopher obviously felt that he had been betrayed. What added to my distress was that Patric refused to communicate on any grounds and I was left with the responsibility not only of the sale but dealing with our belongings plus those of half a dozen other people who had believed they would be safe there.

What seemed so ironic was that a man who had dealt with so many difficult situations, whose profession had been involved with human emotions, and who had for years taught oral communication, could not sort out the practical side of ending a marriage and professional partnership without causing unnecessary problems and pain; and I who had taught so many people to relax had still not learnt to do so myself.

Free of the pressures of the Globe we had enjoyed many happy holidays at the lake but nine years of living alone, especially once the very co-operative neighbours departed, had obviously had their effect on Patric; and I, who had dreaded a solo existence, had to face the fact that this was to be my fate.

Meanwhile I pursued my career as best I could. I had the good fortune to be invited to direct another play in Hawke's Bay and then, in order to renew my acting career, I devised a one-woman show for myself – two contrasting plays which I called *Charlie/Comeback*. This brought me once again to the Globe. There (in 1983), further interesting developments had taken place. The stage had been enlarged and the black-and-white tiles replaced by an overall covering. There was no suggestion of a tarras; black velvet curtains hung from ceiling to floor, but sadly most of the beautiful flock wallpaper in the foyer and auditorium had been painted over with less than satisfactory results.

I gave five wonderfully well-received performances of *Charlie/ Comeback*, of which the *Otago Daily Times* wrote on 27 January 1983:

> her skill as a witty and discerning writer but also as an actress in command of her craft. Her use of stage space, and judgement in characterisation avoided the trap of caricature particularly in her portrayal of ageing Cathy and her equally ageing cat. Some nice touches of humour and pathos here ...

> But the real humour came in Mrs Carey's second play *Comeback* starring the archetypal repertory actress of uncertain years returning to the boards with skirts flying and eyebrows fluttering to impress the local reporter ...

Critiques in the fifty venues I performed in were not dissimilar, apart from a totally damning one, also from Dunedin, written for an Arts Council publication. This, perhaps, accounted for the lack of interest from the professional theatres in Wellington.

While I was in Dunedin members were thinking ahead to ways of celebrating the twenty-fifth anniversary of the Globe, and I was able to sow the seeds for the little book from which I have liberally quoted, which Marian Coxhead put together for the occasion. It was also suggested that, following the success of *Charlie/Comeback*, *A State of Siege* might be revived.

At last my world was looking much more positive.

CHAPTER VXI

From Turbulent Waters to a
Sunny Bank

The Globe is in good hands

᠊ᢀ᠊

In 1984 I was invited to revive *A State of Siege* at the Globe. This time, as well as having assistance from the Community Arts Council, Air New Zealand provided my fares. I was able to stay with good friends, and of course there were royalties for me and Janet Frame.

Not being sure of what technical support I would have, I decided upon an idea I had considered for some time – a shorter version just with Malfred Signal and a narrator. Prior to the Globe season I did a Sunday night performance at Circa Theatre in Wellington with Graeme Thomson, the well-known broadcaster and television presenter, as the narrator. Before the play Graeme and I read a selection of my poems which had been published by Blackberry Press in a little book titled *Over the Hill*. Others, put to music by Nicholas Palmer, were sung very beautifully by Dunedin's Beverley Reid.

When I went south I found the Globe in good heart. Following the retirement of Rodney Kennedy and Mary Middleditch, Rowena Cullen, who had been secretary of the Friends for some years, had taken over the artistic directorship with enthusiasm. Outstanding productions had been Jennifer Barrer's *Strait is the Gate* by the poet R.A.K. Mason, and Mary Middleditch's *The Rocking Cave* by James McNeish; *Confusions* by Alan Ayckbourn directed by Lisa Warrington with Peter McMechan, David Corballis, Harry Love, Barbara Williamson and Hilary Norris in the cast; and Ibsen's *Lady from the Sea* directed by Mary Middleditch and brilliantly costumed by Charmian Smith.

Though much had changed, respect was still paid to our policy of presenting plays for their merit rather the box office appeal, though *Confusions*, I understand, drew capacity houses.

One of the more original projects came from Louise Petherbridge – Shakespeare's *The Tempest* performed by Banraku puppets created by John Middleditch, Louise, Rowena Cullen, Charmian Smith and other members of the Friends committee. With it they toured to

Alexandra and to Christchurch for an arts festival. It was reviewed glowingly in the *Listener* and was shown on the television programme, *Kaleidoscope*.

Another of Louise's 'idiotic suggestions' was to hold a symposium on 'Nothingness and the Void' to test the philosophical possibility or impossibility of discerning 'nothing'.

According to Louise:

> The result was both funny and profound ... The upshot of the symposium for me seemed to be the conclusion outlined by Kosuki Koyama, who made a distinction between the philosophies of East and West. For the West the beginning was the word. For the East the beginning was the void out of which everything was formed.
>
> How apt for the Globe itself – the excitement and challenge of the word and the constant need to create something out of nothing!

Sadly, by the time of my visit Frank Grayson had died, but his memory was still very much alive. With money he left the theatre plus a generous grant from the McMillan Trust through the Dunedin City Council, a new storage room and workshop had been built by the side of the house, and the kitchen vastly improved.

Unhappy with my inner-city cottage in Wellington I began to wonder if I could live in the little flat upstairs, but there had been a fire and the premises were no longer habitable.

Plans for *A State of Siege* were well in hand when I arrived, with a programme to precede it of New Zealand music performed by local artists. The *Dunedin Star Midweek* reported on 29 July 1987:

> Particularly notable were Miranda Adams and Tim Dodd in a violin/piano duet which demonstrated the mastery of their instruments. The music aptly set the scene for Rosalie Carey's adaptation of Janet Frame's *A State of Siege* ... Derisive humour and a sharp wit break the psychological intensity in this play and Carey has an instinct for this sort of humour ... Keith Harrison could not have been a better choice as narrator. His strong resonant voice carries a great respect for its subject and his was a most commanding and sensitive delivery. It was a worthwhile evening of entertainment.

The audio-visual department of the University of Otago filmed the show for the archives.

In 1986 the Globe celebrated its twenty-fifth anniversary and I accepted an invitation to attend. On arrival I was interviewed and photographed by the press and television, and on my suggestion the television team went to Gore and saw Patric. Since I had little news of him through private channels it was good to see him on camera even if he was dressed like Worzel Gummidge. He appeared to be perfectly happy to dig his garden, read books, and act as guide and mentor to a small art gallery that has become very successful.

To celebrate the birthday there was an interesting production of *Romeo and Juliet,* the play that had heralded the opening of the Globe, this time on a cleverly constructed Renaissance set. The director was Peter McMechan of the continuing education unit of the university, who had also been responsible for several other notable productions of classic plays at the Globe. On the Sunday afternoon I gave a poetry reading and the little book *The Globe – a Celebration of 25 Years, 1961– 86* was launched. Regrettably Marian Coxhead, its begetter, and her husband, Leslie, both of whom had done so much for the theatre, were overseas.

In September 1991 the Speech Communication Association Conference was once again held in Dunedin. As I still take some pupils I like to attend these stimulating and informative gatherings whenever possible. A feature of that conference was a literary tour, originally devised by the Historic Places Trust. The tour guides were none other than Keith Harrison and Reg Graham.

It was exciting to recall Keith's delightful performances such as Dionysus in *The Frogs* and Reg's remarkable leap of more than two metres from the tarras onto the stage below when playing Orestes in *Electra,* to say nothing of his dynamic Hamlet in the Burns Hall production.

On the tour we were driven past dwellings and told about such well-known writers as Charles Brasch, Janet Frame, Hone Tuwhare, O.E. Middleton, and James K. Baxter, as well as visual artists and Jack Lovelock, Olympic gold medal winner in 1936.

Then we went to 84 London Street, our first home in Dunedin. On hearing that I was with the party the new owners invited me into the house. When we had moved out, the property was sold to a speculator and converted to a lodging house, but to my immense satisfaction it was now being restored with love and good taste. The conference members had been issued with packed lunches, which we ate in the auditorium of the Globe Theatre, just up the hill from No. 84. Tea and coffee were served by Reg and Keith.

A young women's collective was rehearsing when we arrived. When I was introduced to them it was obvious that the names of Rosalie and Patric Carey had no real relevance. However they asked me to tell them and the teachers a little of how the Globe came into being – a story even I found hard to believe.

Earlier that year the theatre had been closed for six months for extensive alterations, opening again with a successful production of *Twelfth Night*. Renée Taylor, well-known professional playwright, had come to Dunedin for one year as Burns Fellow and like so many others had stayed longer. At the time of my visit, Renée was the Globe's artistic director, from all accounts doing a sterling job. She premièred two of her plays at the Globe and a third, a children's play, was scheduled as the Christmas production for 1993.

Now that the theatre was public property, and with a dynamic person at the helm, grants had come from the Council for Recreation and Sport, Trustees Executors, Perpetual Trustees, and Trustbank Otago as well as those already mentioned, and long-dreamed-of improvements had been made.

The wall between the staircase and the auditorium had been removed. Access was made by narrow staircases on either side of the auditorium, thereby greatly improving the sightlines as well as enlarging the seating capacity. The stupid gaps we had been obliged to introduce were done away with. Another wall, originally created to house the statue of Clio, had also been removed allowing for a much bigger foyer. A huge steel girder replacing the uprights of the old bay window gave a vastly increased, unobstructed acting area. Technical equipment and the heating system had been updated, and a complete new lighting system installed. (The leaks from the roof were reduced, but apparently were not entirely fixed till 1992.) It was all very exciting, but to my horror the whole auditorium, ceiling included, was painted black!

The following year I was invited to adjudicate speech competitions in Oamaru so took the opportunity of making a brief visit to Dunedin. The huge magnolia tree at the front of the house had had its roots supplied with sufficient earth and strategically placed rocks to stop it burrowing further under the building – even in our day the roots had tilted the little studio floor and door to an alarming extent.

The garden had had a face-lift; the old classic urns had been cleaned and painted; the path to the theatre widened, and the exterior of the building was in good repair. Unfortunately, the same could not be said of the house.

In an interview with Raewyn Lippert, for a school assignment, Renée told her:

the Globe reflects the nature of Dunedin well – Dunedin is a place where there are writers, artists, singers and musicians living among the people. They accept that something like writing is a job; they seem to know that you can spend hours and hours and hours writing and they don't think it's anything weird. To them it's quite ordinary to have writers and artists and musicians in their community, so I think the Globe is like a microcosm of Dunedin. The community likes new plays and encourages New Zealand playwrights, especially those residing in Dunedin. The 'Globe' is part of that encouragement, the people there will read new plays and workshop them for the writer if they wish, and generally help them with their work. It's a very good kind of atmosphere here for that reason, very encouraging and supportive.

In March 1993 Renée left to live in Hamilton but she believes the Globe will continue as it always has, as well as 'expanding into all sorts of theatre'.

In January 1997 I made a brief visit to Dunedin and had the good fortune to see Shakespeare's *Coriolanus* directed by Alexander Laube, son of Margaret Laube who has given many splendid performances at the Globe. It was a privilege to see this rarely performed, complex play and to hear even the very young members of the cast speaking the lines with understanding and enjoyment. Marilyn Parker's Volumnia was, as might be expected, a vocally rich, well-rounded performance.

The concluding paragraph of Raewyn Lippert's assignment states:

The 'Globe' has remained true to itself and has encouraged the presentation of the unusual, the bizarre and the experimental. Sometimes the productions have been failures but there have been others that have been dazzling, mind-catching and brilliant to balance the record.

Looking through the list of plays only as far as 1986 I am amazed at the number and their quality, and wonder how many theatres can boast such a record?

The current President of the Friends of the Globe is Beth Rask who came to our production of *Medea* when she was twelve years old and maintains the Globe has been a spiritual home for her and many others. Recently she told me that she has an energetic enthusiastic committee and that their *The Merchant of Venice* directed by Donald Hope-Evans enjoyed full houses, with hundreds turned away. 'Who said Shakespeare didn't put bums on seats?' she said. 'The cast could only manage one extra performance but we could have played for another week!'

There were seven productions at the Globe in 1998, including an extremely well revived *King Lear*, and Oscar Wilde's stylish play *Lady Windermere's Fan*. The planned programme for 1999 is no less than eleven productions, including Wilde's *The Importance of Being Earnest*, comedy by Terence (a classic playwright), a new play by James Hadley, my *Modus Vivendi* and dramatisation of Janet Frame's *A State of Siege*, and a production by the Globe Young Peoples' Theatre which operates throughout the year under the direction of Marama Grant, Lyndon Hood and Julie Harris. As well as this there are plans for saving the old house, and restoring the theatre's two-tiered stage. It would seem that Renée was not far wrong.

Finally, an update on the Carey family. Patric appears to be at peace with the world. After bumming around overseas for several years Christopher became a professional potter in Japan, but wishing to expand his artistic horizons took three jobs in order to finance himself through the course at the Emily Carr School of Art in Vancouver, and graduated with flying colours. He married a talented fellow student, Sandra Storey. After a successful year teaching and exhibiting – the *Vancouver Times* described their work as the most interesting that year – they sailed to New Zealand in a thirty-five-foot yacht in which they lived in the Town Basin in Whangarei until they were able to buy an old house in which to accommodate a new baby, who has become my pride and joy.

They have a half share with two glass-blowers in an exciting three-dimensional gallery, *Burning Issues*. As well as continuing with their own creative ceramic work and taking their turn in the gallery, they both teach and Christopher is working towards a Master of Fine Arts Diploma at the Auckland Institute of Technology.

After many years in Australia where she went originally to attend the Victoria College of the Arts, Belinda, her partner and two children returned to New Zealand. Belinda took the third-year course at the Conservatorium of Music in Wellington, majoring in recorder playing. This was followed by a year at the College of Education. She is now teaching at Nayland College in Nelson, Head of Performing Arts. In 1997 her school quartet won the Westpac prize and with her drama class she directed Aristophanes' *The Frogs* in which she had appeared as a very little frog when she was about three years old. Shadows of Patric Carey linger on. Belinda also plays bassoon in the local orchestra, which she and a friend managed to have promoted to professional status.

As for me, though I have 'run my three score years and ten' I have no thoughts of retiring. In April 1994 I went to England to see the reconstructed Globe Theatre and the handing over of the beautiful embroidered hangings, sponsored by the Wellington Shakespeare Society, of which I had become a keen active member. The building was far from finished but it was exciting to be there.

On my return I spent a few days in Auckland, and Christopher and Sandra came down for the weekend. I heard that my old admirer had been seriously ill, so we decided to go and see him. He was still tall and handsome, in fact snow white hair made him look more distinguished than ever. He was so delighted I went back next day and on my return to Wellington there were flowers and regular phone calls begging me to come to Auckland. I answered his invitations a couple of times. He was very frail but I agreed, after all those years, to marry him.

I had already booked to attend a voice conference in Auckland and while I was there my old friend was involved in a motor accident. He survived for only three days. Mercifully I was with him when he died.

I had already begun packing and making arrangements for my pupils – the best group I had had for years. I had always claimed I would not choose to end my days in my sunless Wellington cottage and when Christopher and Sandra suggested I might like to live in the winterless North the idea seemed mad, but worth considering. I spent four days with them on the yacht and before leaving had bought a house and put my cottage on the market. It sold within a week.

I am now enjoying the warmth and quiet of a small puddle – Whangarei. I have a pleasant home with a ridiculously large but productive garden. I have published my third small book of poems, and *Operation Laughter: Sick jokes, stories and reminiscences* as a fundraiser for the Cancer Society. I have also arranged a number of programmes of poetry, prose and music – two of them in costume – to raise funds for various organisations. There was also an interesting programme in which I narrated an Irish legend and *The Story of Baba* accompanied on harp and piano respectively by Dorothea Franchi. We performed both in Warkworth, where Dorothea now lives, and in Whangarei.

I belong to three stimulating writers' groups, the Choral Society and the Repertory Society and had *Tomorrow's Coming – an Irreverent Peace Play* produced at the Octagon Theatre in 1996. In 1998, Stuart

Devenie workshopped and directed one of my three-act plays – *Modus Vivendi* – a very exciting project. I have appeared in a local melodrama and have had an amusing little part in *Shortland Street*. I have made some wonderful friends and found to my great surprise that people away up here have heard about the little theatre in Dunedin.

After all the trauma the family has been through, I feel confident about the future and we all of us look back without regret for having lived so long with a theatre in the house.

Plays Performed at the Globe

All of the early plays were Rosalie and Patric Carey Productions; others were the work of guest producers including Pamela Pow, Mary Middleditch, Ian Ralston and John Casserley. This list does not include children's theatre productions.

Pre-Globe Productions

	1957	*Director*
Medea	Euripides	P. Carey

	1958	
The Oresteia	Aeschylus	P. Carey
A Sleep of Prisoners	Fry	P. Carey
Hamlet	Shakespeare	P. Carey

	1959	
The Women of Troy	Euripides	P. Carey
Oedipus Rex	Sophocles	P. Carey
Antigone	Sophocles	P. Carey
The Maids	Genet	P. Carey
Waiting for Godot	Beckett	P. Carey
The Chairs	Ionesco	P. Carey
Blind Man's Tale	Anne de Roo	P. Carey
The Frogs	Aristophanes	P. Carey

	1960	
The Frogs	Aristophanes	P. Carey
Alcestis	Euripides	P. Carey
The Bald Prima Donna	Ionesco	P. Carey
The Duchess of Malfi	Webster	P. Carey
J.B.	MacLeish	P. Carey
The Cave Dwellers	Saroyan	P. Carey
The Taming of the Shrew	Shakespeare	P. Carey
Miss Julie	Strindberg	P. Carey
Don Bludgeon was a Puppet	Lorca	P. Carey

	1961	
The Birds	Aristophanes	P. Carey
Electra	Sophocles, adapt. de Roo	P. Carey
John Gabriel Borkman	Ibsen	P. Carey

Globe Theatre Productions

	1961	
Romeo and Juliet	Shakespeare	P. Carey
Endgame	Beckett	P. Carey
The Glass Menagerie	Williams	P. Carey
The Lesson	Ionesco	P. Carey

Three Actors and Their Drama	Ghelderode	P. Carey
Othello	Shakespeare	P. Carey
Hedda Gabler	Ibsen	P. Carey

1962

Maria Marten	Anon	P. Carey
The American Dream	Albee	P. Carey
Arms and the Man	Shaw	P. Carey
Little Eyolf	Ibsen	P. Carey
Under the Sycamore Tree	Spewack	A. Stephens
The Broken Pitcher	von Kleist	E. Herd
She Stoops to Conquer	Goldsmith	P. Carey
Huis Clos	Sartre	P. Carey
The New Tenant	Ionesco	P. Carey
The Potting Shed	Greene	M. Middleditch
Three Sisters	Chekhov	P. Carey
The Stranger	Camus	P. Carey
The Oresteia	Aeschylus	P. Carey

1963

Agamemnon	Aeschylus	P. Carey
Maria Marten	Anon	P. Carey
Lysistrata	Aristophanes	P. Carey
Roots	Wesker	P. Pow
Chicken Soup with Barley	Wesker	P. Carey
I'm talking about Jerusalem	Wesker	R. Carey
A Month in the Country	Turgenev	P. Carey
The Fire Raisers	Frisch	E. Herd
A Modern Man at Breakfast	Guyan	A. Guyan
Conversations With a Golliwog	Guyan	A. Stephens
Lady Precious Stream	Hsuing	M. Middleditch
Orisons	Arrabal	P. Carey
Fando and Lis	Arrabal	P. Carey
The Cherry Orchard	Chekhov	P. Carey
Rosmersholm	Ibsen	P. Carey
The Government Inspector	Gogol	P. Carey

1964

The Night of the Iguana	Williams	P. Carey
Hamlet	Shakespeare	P. Carey
Happy Days	Beckett	P. Carey
Shadow and Substance	Carroll	A. Stephens
The Collection	Pinter	P. Pow
The Lover	Pinter	M. Noonan
In Good King Charles' Golden Days	Shaw	P. Carey
The Government Inspector	Gogol	W. Vlassov
Suddenly Last Summer	Williams	P. Carey
Something Unspoken	Williams	P. Carey
Uncle Vanya	Chekhov	P. Carey

1965

'The Escape', 'The Magic Bowl'	revue	R. Carey
Hamlet	Shakespeare	P. Carey
Under Milk Wood	Thomas	R. Carey
Orpheus Descending	Williams	P. Carey
The Playboy of the Western World	Synge	P. Carey
The Creditors	Strindberg	P. Pow
The Stronger	Strindberg	P. Pow
Who's Afraid of Virginia Woolf?	Albee	P. Carey
The Maids	Genet	P. Carey

The Frogs	Aristophanes	P. Carey
The Seagull	Chekhov	P. Carey
One Way Pendulum	Simpson	R. Carey

1966

The Seagull	Chekhov	P. Carey
One Way Pendulum	Simpson	R. Carey
Excerpts from Great Plays		R. Carey
Waiting for Godot	Beckett	P. Carey
Juno and the Paycock	O'Casey	P. Carey
The House of Bernarda Alba	Lorca	P. Freeman
Saint Joan	Shaw	P. Carey
Tartuffe	Molière	R. Stone
The Burnt Flower Bed	Betti	P. Carey
The Petulant Puppeteer	Spears, de Roo, Skinner	R. Carey
Hotel Paradiso	Feydeau	P. Pow
Three Sisters	Chekhov	P. Carey
The Dark is Light Enough	Fry	Middleditch
Marat/Sade	Weiss	P. Carey

1967

Excerpts from Great Plays		R. Carey
Women of Troy	Euripides	R. Carey
The Burnt Flower Bed	Betti	P. Carey
Three Sisters	Chekhov	R. Carey
Between These Four Walls	Revue	I. Ralston
The Master Builder	Ibsen	P. Carey
Marat/Sade	Weiss	P. Carey
Ladies' Day	Aristophanes	P. Carey
Faust	Goethe	J. Dawson
Recital of Modern Dance		J. Casserley
The Band Rotunda	Baxter	P. Carey
Act Without Words	Beckett	J. Casserley
The Bacchae	Euripides	J. Casserley, I. Ralston
The Sore-Footed Man	Baxter	P. Carey
The Woman	Baxter	J. Casserley
The Apple Cart	Shaw	P. Carey, J. Casserley
'Look Back in Anguish'	sketches and parodies	
The Bureaucrat	Baxter	P. Carey
The Axe and the Mirror	Baxter	J. Casserley
An Evening with Baxter, Trio	Baxter	P. Carey, J. Casserley
A History of Costume and Manners		R. Carey
The Devil and Mr Mulcahy	Baxter	P. Carey
The Cross	Baxter	J. Casserley
Loose Boards and Seagulls	Olds	P. Carey, J. Casserley
The Dragon	Schwartz	P. Carey
Christmas in the Market Place	Gheon	I. Ralston
'The Visit'	R. Carey	R. Carey

1968

The Band Rotunda	Baxter	P. Carey
The Cross	Baxter	J. Casserley
Loose Boards and Seagulls	Olds	P. Carey, J. Casserley
The Sore-Footed Man	Baxter	P. Carey
The Woman	Baxter	J. Casserley
The Bureaucrat	Baxter	P. Carey
The Axe and The Mirror	Baxter	J. Casserley
Endgame	Beckett	J. Casserley
The Deal and *The Long Wait*	Tourelle)	
The Rendezvous and *The World Is*	Baxter)	R. Carey

The Winter's Tale	Shakespeare	H. Smith
Twelfth Night	Shakespeare	P. Carey
Electra	Sophocles	J. McConnell
Tiny Alice	Albee	P. Carey
Antigone	Sophocles	R. Carey
Too True to be Good	Shaw	R. Carey
Antigone	Anouilh	P. Carey, E. Durning
The Good Woman of Setzuan	Brecht	I. Fraser, B. Einhorn, M. Herd, R. Wilson
Dancers and Ladies		I. Ralston
The Cherry Orchard	Chekhov	P. Carey
Mr O'Dwyer's Dancing Party	Baxter	P. Carey
The Duchess of Malfi	Webster	P. Carey

1969

The Bald Prima Donna	Ionesco	G. Wood
Mr O'Dwyer's Dancing Party	Baxter	P. Carey
The Duchess of Malfi	Webster	P. Carey
The Day Flanagan Died	Baxter	P. Carey
Endgame	Beckett	P. Carey, I. Ralston
Classical Indian Dance Recital		
The Four Seasons	Wesker	I. Ralston
Jazz Concert		
Shelley – or The Idealist	Ann Jellicoe	P. Pow
Lines to a Mock Turtle	Warren Dibble	P. Carey
A Delicate Balance	Albee	P. Carey
The Pied Piper, a Children's Opera	Browning (*arr. Fleming*)	M. Fleming, R. Carey
Andorra	Frisch	B. Evans
Woyzeck	Büchner	J. Dawson
The Spirit and the Flesh	Browning	H. Smith, I. Fraser
Question Time	John Smith	P. Carey
The Harmfulness of Tobacco – A Lecture	Chekhov	I. Ralston
Evening of Guitar Music and Poetry		
The Father	Strindberg	P. Carey
American Hurrah	van Itallie	I. Ralston
Black Champagne	revue	R. Carey, S. Mackenzie

1970

A Sleep of Prisoners	Fry	P. Carey
The Father	Strindberg	P. Carey
The Spirit and the Flesh	Browning	H. Smith, I. Fraser
Character Sketches from Browning	Browning	R. Carey
The Temptations of Oedipus	Baxter	P. Carey
Baroque Ensemble	NZ Baroque Players	
Easter	Strindberg	P. Carey
Duet for Two Actresses	excerpts	H. Eggleton, M. MacMahon, A. Phillips
The Family Reunion	Eliot	P. Carey
Ardèle ou La Marguerite	Anouilh	R. Collins
Uncle Vanya	Chekhov	P. Carey, M. Seifert
Hippolytus	Euripides	R. Carey
The Sea Kings Daughter	M. Harding	R. Carey
A State of Siege	J. Frame/R. Carey	I. Ralston
Under Milk Wood	Thomas	M. Seifert

1971

Choephoroe	Aeschylus	R. Carey
A State of Siege	J. Frame/R. Carey	I. Ralston
Under Milk Wood	Thomas	R. Carey
She Stoops to Conquer	Goldsmith	P. Carey

You Never Can Tell	Shaw	P. Carey
The Conquest of Princess Turandot	Hildesheimer	M. Herd
La Malade Imaginaire	Molière	M. Anderson
Hamlet 2000	Shakespeare	P. Carey
Othello	Shakespeare	I. Ralston
Oktoberfest		
A Hole Whirled in a Cup of Mince	revue	J. Mack
The Cocktail Party	Eliot	P. Carey, A. Walker
Blest Pair of Sirens	revue	
Dance Boy for Rain	A. Loney	I. Ralston

1972

Who's Afraid of Virginia Woolf?	Albee	P. Carey, N. Dolamore
The Man of Destiny	Shaw	R. Carey
Krapp's Last Tape	Beckett	I. Ralston
Dance Boy for Rain	A. Loney	I. Ralston
Much Ado About Nothing	Shakespeare	P. Carey
Exiles	Joyce	P. Carey, W. Bloomfield
Appendix to Captain Cook's Voyage	Giraudoux	R. Carey
Saints' Day	Whiting	P. Carey, R. Cullen
The Cherry Orchard	Chekhov	N. Dolamore, P. Carey
Richard II (Allen Hall)	Shakespeare	I. Ralston
You'll Come to Love Your Sperm Test (Allen Hall)	Antrobus	T. Bryan
Penny for a Song	Whiting	P. Carey, T. Bryan
The Hollow Crown	John Barton	B. Robertson
Baroque Concert	Local musicians	K. Dawson
Globe Theatre School Production		R. Carey, S. Dunlop

1973

Marching Song	Whiting	P. Carey
Ring-a-Ring-a-Rosie	Schnitzler	J. Dawson
'Nam	Mann	A. Curreri
Next Time I'll Sing to You	Saunders	I. Garner
The Horse	Julius Hay	R. Carey
The Philanthropist	C. Hampton	H. Elliott
Cat on a Hot Tin Roof	Williams	M. Middleditch
The Confidential Clerk	Eliot	P. Carey
Landscape	Pinter	L. Petherbridge
Silence	Pinter	L. Petherbridge
The Devils	Whiting	P. Carey (*last production*)
A Feast of Fools	revue	R. Carey, S. Dunlop
Homage to Ilma Maude Levy	revue	J. Bailey

Artists shown at the Globe

Paintings, prints, sculpture and ceramics exhibited by the following artists:

Tanya Ashken, Doreen Blumhardt, Barry Brickell, John Brown, Len Castle, John Coley, Charlton Edgar, Tom Esplin, David Graham, Jeffrey Harris, Ralph Hotere, Michael Illingworth, Beryl Jowett, Bill Mackay, Para Matchitt, Donald McAra, Colin McCahon, John Middleditch, Selwyn Muru, Els Noordhof, Michael Smither, Marilyn Webb.

Index

An asterisk preceding the name of a play denotes that all page references are to productions at the Globe Theatre; similarly, an asterisk preceding a page reference denotes a production at the Globe.

Campton, David 138, 139
Camus, Albert: *The Stranger 45-6
Carey, Belinda 26-7, 34, 47, 60, 68, 80, 100, 120, 127, 134, 141, 143, 144, 147, 154
Carey, Christopher 18, 20, 34, 50, 58, 68, 71, 72, 75, 85, 89, 96, 116, 120, 127, 131, 137, 138, 141, 143, 147, 153-5
Carey, Patric: background in UK 12-16; aspirations 12; marries Rosalie 14; CAS tour 17, in Wellington 17-19; adjudicator 18ff; producer, Dunedin Repertory 19-22; Greek drama 21, 24-6; moves to 104 London St 9, 24; Southern Comedy Players 22-3, 24; aspirations for NZ theatre 24; Rosalie and Patric Carey Productions 24-9, 31, 157; builds two-tier stages 27; new wave theatre 28-9, 45ff; building the Globe 32-5; opening production 35-8; plays Old Capulet 36; first year 39-45; Wesker trilogy 49; first Chekhov production 51; Ibsen production invited to Christchurch 51-2; extending the Globe 56-60; 19th-century Hamlet 60-1; Uncle Vanya 63; love of music 64, 138; pleasure in producing plays 65, 102, 145; joins in Globe teaching programme 67; arranging exhibitions 67; teaching at Knox College 70; Who's Afraid of Virginia Woolf? 75-6; Saint Joan 78; decision-making with RC 78, 105; opposes commercialism of Arts Council 85; threatens to close Globe 85; and Baxter 89-97, 115; suggests Baxter takes Greeks for his model 92; second production Godot 107-8; teaching at seminary 108; rehearses at Mahinerangi 109; strained relations with RC 105, 112; health 112, 116, 125; sells Globe to Friends 113-14; contract with Friends 113-14; last production before handover 115; directs You Never Can Tell in Christchurch 120; directs Hamlet 2000 123-4; directs Eliot plays 125; directs and tours Who's Afraid ... 127-8; success of Exiles 129; part in Richard II 131; directs Whiting plays 133-5; final production at Globe, 135; retirement 135; reflections 136-7; music commissioned by 138; breakdown of marriage 146-7; at Gore 147, 151, 153; Globe productions directed by 157-61; relationship with casts 56, 63, 102, 103-4, 133-4, 135
Carey, Rosalie (née Seddon) early career 10-15; marriage 14; arrives NZ 17; CAS tour 17; in Wellington 17-19; birth of son 18; to Dunedin 19; 104 London St 9, 24; early productions Greek drama 21, 24-6, 139; Southern Comedy Players

22-3, 24; Rosalie and Patric Carey Productions 24-9, 31, 157; birth of daughter 26; founds the Globe with PC 31ff see also Globe Theatre; duties in first production 36; directs I'm Talking about Jerusalem 49-50; enlarging Globe 56-60; directing university drama 64, 108, 128; develops classes at Globe 67ff; directs One Way Pendulum 77; decision-making with PC 78; casting 77-8; directs Too True to be Good 107; directs The Simpleton of the Unexpected Isles 107; strained relations with PC 105, 112; agrees to sell Globe 113; contract with Friends 113-14; concern for PC's health 64, 116, 125; dramatises/performs A State of Siege 116-18; health 127, 131, 143, 145, 146-7; directs Supplement to Cook's Voyage 130; trip to UK 136, 141-2; at RNZ 144-5; breakdown of marriage 146-7; directs own plays at Globe 145, 147; revives Siege at Circa and Globe 149; at Globe 25th celebrations 150-1; living in Whangarei 155; Globe productions directed by 158-60; OTHER THEATRICAL WORK: adjudicating 18, 72, 80, 84, 152; costume design/ wardrobe 43-4, 61, 65, 75, 114, 119; teaching 11, 18, 20-1, 24, 26-7, 35, 40, 64, 65, 67-74, 76, 109, 120, 127, 141, 151; PLAYS: dramatisation of Frame, A State of Siege 116-18, 139, 148, 149-50; Black Champagne (revue, with Shirley Mackenzie) 109; Charlie/Comeback (one-woman show) 147-8; Edendale Station 145-6; I Can Give You a Bed 119, 145; Modus Vivendi 155; Tomorrow's Coming – An Irreverent Peace Play 155
Carey/Mackenzie: *Black Champagne (revue) 109
Carnegie, David 10, 38, 45, 83, 97
Caselberg, John 139
Casserley, Barbara 80, 93
Casserley, John 69, 80, 84, 93, 94, 105
Castle, Len 47, 138
Cattell, Pauline 119
Central Theatre 55
Chance, Kristin 40
Chekhov 91; *The Cherry Orchard 51, 53, 95-6; *The Seagull 62; *Three Sisters 80; *Uncle Vanya 62, 63, 116
Children of the Globe Theatre 67-8, 100; *The Petulant Puppeteer 68
Christchurch Repertory Society 120
Circa Theatre 149
Clare, Peter 60, 69, 101
Clausen, William 139
Clifford, Graeme 22
Coley, John 138
Community Arts Council 118, 149